12/05

ASHE Higher Education Report: Volume 31, Number 4
Kelly Ward, Lisa E. Wolf-Wendel, Series Editors

D0939970

Professionalizing Graduate Education

The Master's Degree in the Marketplace

Judith Glazer-Raymo

Professionalizing Graduate Education: The Master's Degree in the Marketplace
Judith Glazer-Raymo
ASHE Higher Education Report: Volume 31, Number 4
Kelly Ward, Lisa Wolf-Wendel, Series Editors

ISSN 1551-6970   electronic ISSN 1554-6306   ISBN 0-7879-8361-6

The ASHE Higher Education Report is part of the Jossey-Bass Higher and Adult Education Series and is published six times a year by Wiley Subscription Services, Inc., A Wiley Company, at Jossey-Bass, 989 Market Street, San Francisco, California 94103-1741.

For subscription information, see the Back Issue/Subscription Order Form in the back of this volume.

CALL FOR PROPOSALS: Prospective authors are strongly encouraged to contact Kelly Ward (kaward@wsu.edu) or Lisa Wolf-Wendel (lwolf@ku.edu). See "About the ASHE Higher Education Report Series" in the back of this volume.

Visit the Jossey-Bass Web site at **www.josseybass.com.**

Printed in the United States of America on acid-free recycled paper.

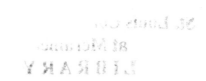

Advisory Board

The ASHE Higher Education Report Series is sponsored by the Association for the Study of Higher Education (ASHE), which provides an editorial advisory board of ASHE members.

Contents

Executive Summary

The master's degree exemplifies the diversity and complexity of graduate education in the twenty-first century. As a predoctoral, intermediate, or terminal credential, its conferral validates successful completion of a course of study in the arts and sciences or in the professions. This study traces the extraordinary growth and multiple trajectories of master's education in the context of a culture of professionalization. Theoretical studies of the restructuring of knowledge across disciplinary boundaries provide a conceptual vocabulary for understanding the multiple meanings of academic and professional degrees and their pivotal role in American higher education.

What Is the Current Status of the Master's Degree?

Three times as many institutions award master's degrees as doctorates. In 2001–2002, 482,118 master's degrees were awarded in twenty-nine fields and 426 subfields, an increase of 60 percent since 1982–1983. A disproportionate share—53 percent—was conferred in education and business, compared with almost 11.8 percent in the sciences and engineering, 6 percent in the social sciences, and 2.3 percent in the humanities. By 2012, the National Center for Education Statistics projects that 556,000 master's degrees will be awarded. To contextualize these developments, this study analyzes five fully professionalized fields, nine arts and science disciplines now undergoing professionalization, and three interdisciplinary fields now being reconceptualized. Degree proliferation accelerates as graduate and professional schools seek new markets in which to promote their programs and services. A variety of innovative practices now make it difficult to devise typologies that alternatively categorize master's degrees as basic or advanced, research or practitioner, intermediate or terminal, general or specialized, preprofessional or professional, fast track or multiyear, executive or entry level, asynchronous or classroom based, dual or combined.

What Are the Major Issues?

Governing boards, accrediting agencies, and professional associations issue periodic calls for "reform." In their admonitions for quality control, accountability, professional standards, and ethical codes of conduct, these bodies reflect the voices of myriad stakeholders, students, faculty, alumni, and employers among them. This monograph pays particular attention to initiatives supporting innovation and change in graduate education, the growth of for-profit providers, the profitability of online and distance learning systems, industrial consortia and partnerships, and the creation of standardized degrees through, for example, the creation of a European higher education area involving forty national systems.

What Is the Future Trajectory of Master's Education?

Four mechanisms will continue to propel the professionalization of master's education and its pivotal role in the marketplace: technological advances, global partnerships, mandates for accountability, and the permeability of disciplinary and institutional boundaries. Whereas the arts and sciences had been central to the university mission throughout the twentieth century, professional programs now predominate throughout the degree hierarchy. The geographic proximity of universities and workplaces, part-time and weekend courses, employer subsidies, and virtual campuses further enhance the marketability of the master's degree. This study concludes with recommendations for extending departmental and institutional dialogues on the future of higher education to clienteles inside and outside the academy, reframing questions about the principles and purposes of master's education and addressing the ambiguous relationship of academic and professional degrees, the deficiencies of federal taxonomies and classification systems, the impact of profitability in competitive global environments, and the overriding influence of credentialism in contemporary culture.

Foreword

In the past two decades, significant changes have taken place in graduate and professional education in the United States; developments in the master's degree are emblematic of its transformation. The role and significance of the master's degree as a marketable credential provides an array of choices to students in the United States that exceeds previously available options, largely due to the technological advances that now make it possible to earn a wide range of accredited master's degrees through remote links to universities and colleges in professional and academic disciplines and in interdisciplinary fields. In this monograph, Judith Glazer-Raymo analyzes the depth and breadth of master's education, drawing on the extant literature on graduate and professional education, national databases, extensive fieldwork, and participation in symposia and forums. The result is a comprehensive overview and analysis of the current status of master's education in the academic "marketplace."

The master's degree, unlike associate, baccalaureate, or doctoral degrees, occupies a critical juncture in the degree hierarchy at the intersection of undergraduate and graduate education, professional and academic fields, and knowledge production and applications. It has supplanted the baccalaureate as the requisite credential for gaining access and recognition in numerous professions. Given its exponential growth rate and prominence, it is important to reflect on its role and significance. Glazer-Raymo provides a rich resource for scholars, practitioners, employers, and the many stakeholders concerned with current and future directions of graduate and professional education.

In 1986, Glazer-Raymo wrote what was then the definitive study of the master's degree: an ASHE-ERIC Report entitled *The Master's Degree: Tradition,*

Diversity, and Innovation. Written in a decade of fiscal retrenchment and accountability mandates, innovation was occurring at the periphery rather than the center of graduate education. Nevertheless, Glazer-Raymo prompted her readers to think creatively about its diversity and its potential for future development. Twenty years later, she has written another definitive study of master's education. But her work is more than an update or road map to understanding the degree. Rather, it artfully details the history and evolution of master's programs, framing their advancement within the context of professionalization and the sociology of knowledge, delineating the nuances of graduate education in academic disciplines, interdisciplines, and professional fields. Her study also addresses the significance of American colleges and universities in exporting models of master's education to international audiences, and the far-reaching changes now occurring in European higher education.

Glazer-Raymo takes the position that the "master's degree has become a pivotal force in the economic growth of the university." As higher education continues to evolve, this monograph provides an invaluable resource for college and university constituencies—administrators, faculty, students, and trustees—in making informed decisions regarding the current status and future directions of their master's programs. For government agencies and private foundations who devise policies that support graduate and professional education, it provides the opportunity to consider increases in financial support for master's students and the master's curriculum, particularly in liberal arts and science, which are central to the mission of the university. For professional associations and state agencies, it provides insights regarding issues of accountability and quality control.

The author concludes by urging academic leaders to consider a number of unresolved critical issues. She poses complex questions about the degree's relationship to the marketplace, and urges ongoing dialogues about future trajectories for graduate education.

Kelly Ward
Washington State University

Acknowledgments

Many colleagues have contributed generously to my efforts, sharing knowledge about their disciplines and their views on master's education. I thank Jesse Ausubel, Eleanor Babco, Michael Teitelbaum, and Sheila Tobias for their leadership and support of graduate education in the sciences. I also express my appreciation to Leslie Sims and Peter Syverson at the Council of Graduate Schools, who have given me such valuable feedback over the past two years. To the many individuals in professional associations, universities, and government agencies, I extend my thanks for their willingness to meet with me, respond to my requests for information, and take part in symposia: Charles Ambler, Trudy Banta, Ursula Bechert, Nicholas Claudy, Stella Coakley, Robert Corbett, Gregory Dewey, Fred Fox, Cristina Giannetto, Jeannine Kantz, Philip Katz, Lisa Lattuca, Thomas Lenox, Karen Ogulnick, Thomas Scott, Giancarlo Spinelli, Frances Stage, Bonnie Stall, and Eileen Weiss. I also thank Kristen Cohen, Andrew LeGrand, and Winston Thompson for their technical assistance. I express appreciation to Kelly Ward, the ASHE Series coeditor; Matthew Hoover, Jossey-Bass production editor; and the three anonymous reviewers for their detailed and highly useful comments on the manuscript. Last but not least, I thank my spouse, Robert Raymo, who has willingly served as a sounding board and critic throughout this project.

Conceptualizing the Master's Degree

T RADITIONAL CONCEPTUALIZATIONS OF ACADEMIC AND PROFESSIONAL DEGREES have designated the use of various titles to be conferred on students in academic, professional, and vocational programs upon their satisfactory completion of coursework. As universities and colleges and their academic programs have grown in number and diversity in the past half century, the content, structure, and meaning of academic degrees have also expanded. Master's education exemplifies the complexity of this process. Throughout its long history, the master's degree has been variously characterized by graduate faculty and deans as an intermediate degree signifying its location following the baccalaureate and preceding the doctorate, as a "predoctoral" or "intermediate" year of graduate school or stepping stone to the doctorate, as a "terminal" degree for those concluding their formal education, or as a "consolation prize" denoting failure to advance to Ph.D. candidacy or completion. The use of the words *intermediate* and *terminal* indicates placement of the master's degree within a continuum of officially recognized titles such as the Master of Business Administration (M.B.A.) or the Master of Fine Arts (M.F.A.), conferred on students upon completion of a program of academic or professional study and certifying their qualification to practice in a professional field. These multiple meanings of the master's degree reflect a number of trends, both institutional and global, that are altering the purposes of higher and postsecondary education and changing the trajectory of graduate and professional education. Moreover, master's degrees in the United States may be awarded by doctoral/research or master's institutions, consistent with the Carnegie classification system that was recently revised (Carnegie

Foundation, 2001). Six categories are used to classify the U.S. system of higher education: doctoral/research universities—extensive and intensive, master's colleges and universities (formerly comprehensive I and II), baccalaureate (liberal arts and general), associate's colleges, and a broad category of specialized and technical institutions. At least 148 institutions (3.8 percent) fall into the category "doctoral/research universities—extensive" based on conferral of fifty or more doctorates per year in at least fifteen disciplines, another 2.9 percent are "doctoral/research universities—intensive" based on conferral of at least ten doctorates annually in three or more disciplines, and 16 percent are master's colleges and universities offering a wide range of bachelor's degrees and twenty or more master's per year. Baccalaureate colleges comprise 15 percent, associate's colleges 42 percent, and specialized institutions 20 percent (Carnegie Foundation, 2001, p. 7).[1]

By 2001, 15.9 million students were enrolled in 4,074 American colleges and universities; 2.2 million were enrolled in graduate and first-professional programs, more than half of them—1.4 million—at the master's level. Graduate enrollments rose about 38 percent between 1985 and 2001; first-professional enrollments increased 13 percent between 1990 and 2001 (Snyder, Tan, and Hoffman, 2004). More than 1.8 million degrees were awarded in 2001, 482,118 of them at the master's level and 308,647 at the first-professional level. Three times as many institutions award master's degrees (1,508) as doctorates (548). The National Center for Education Statistics (NCES) projects that in 2013, 556,000 master's degrees will be awarded (Gerald and Hussar, 2003).[2]

This study provides analyses of the meaning of these numbers in terms of the multiplicity of clienteles enrolling in traditional and innovative master's programs, the factors that have historically motivated their participation, and current and future trajectories for the growth and diversity of master's education. Theoretical studies of the restructuring of disciplinary knowledge and the extent of its professionalization provide a conceptual vocabulary for understanding the complex factors and manifold mechanisms that contribute to its development in the professions and in the liberal arts and science. The next chapter provides some historical background about the master's degree. The historical exposition of master's education, however, tells only one part of the story, and that chapter plus the next one contextualizes the author's analysis of master's education (Klein, 1993, 2000); Nowotny, Scott and Gibbons, 2001) and its professionalization in the university (Abbott, 2001; Brint, 1994; Collins, 1990). Data about the changing demographics of master's education—the new generation of graduate students who now account for almost half a million part-time and full-time enrollments in master's programs—are also included.

Professional master's programs are gaining impetus from a number of forces—globalization, privatization, accountability, and demographic changes in the composition of graduate students. The core of the book contextualizes these developments and contains descriptions of five fields that exemplify fully professionalized programs (accounting, business, education, engineering, and public administration). A separate chapter is devoted to the natural sciences (bioscience, geoscience, chemistry, and physics) where the master's degree plays a more prominent role, and another discussion reviews mixed trends in the humanities and social sciences where professionalization has assumed multiple meanings in some disciplines and, in the same institutions, interdisciplinary degrees are promoted as "nonprofessional." Interdisciplinary fields focus on the early examples of American Studies and liberal studies, now being reconceptualized to encompass disparate fields, and the emerging but vibrant field of women's studies.

The last two chapters look at some of the trends in master's education and summarize the findings of this study.

Throughout, this study takes the position that the master's degree has become a pivotal force in the economic growth of the university. Operating at the interstices of academic degrees, it contributes to the discourse of interdisciplinary innovation and organizational change. Its compatibility with emergent institutional forms and its short-term nature enhance its potential for development by master's and doctoral-granting institutions, whether they are public, private, or for-profit, operating in traditional or nontraditional modes of teaching and learning. Four mechanisms that will continue to propel the professionalized trajectory of master's education relate to technological advances, global initiatives, quality control and accountability, and the convergence of academic and professional fields across disciplinary, departmental, and institutional boundaries.

An earlier monograph points out a number of disincentives to restructuring master's education in a period of fiscal retrenchment (Glazer, 1986). Innovation and change occurred primarily at the margins in undergraduate and continuing education programs, experimental colleges, and Universities Without Walls. This customary practice is no longer the norm. External and joint degrees, cooperative education, interuniversity consortia, multidisciplinary programs, and online and distance learning have been institutionalized and, in many fields, are replacing more traditional models of graduate and professional education. Addressing the challenges implicit in this realignment of academic structures and intellectual content will contribute to a more informed dialogue on the outcomes of graduate and professional education among faculty, students, practitioners, and academic leaders.

The Evolution of the Master's Degree

THE MASTER'S DEGREE IS EVOLVING as an entrepreneurial credential with the potential to alter the direction of graduate education in the liberal arts and sciences as well as in the professions. Beyond the sciences, the predominance of professional master's degrees in the social and behavioral sciences, in the humanities, and in specialized fields indicates not only a different mission for graduate education but also a new direction for the production of knowledge, one that is restructured across disciplinary and professional boundaries and is more responsive to the marketplace than to traditional academic environments. The ideology of professionalism that had distinguished occupations by their location in a hierarchy of prestige, income, power, or control over production, elevating them with the same broad quantity of imputed skill, prestige, and education to professional status, no longer exists; moreover, the security and autonomy of the professional is no longer assured (Leicht and Fennell, 2001). We need look no farther than changes occurring in the field of medicine to recognize that hospital and medical school mergers, managed care, and off-shore medical degree mills are changing the nature of what had been considered the archetype of status professions.

The academic degree is both cultural artifact and eponymous symbol of American postsecondary education, "part of the dogma through which the academic system legitimizes its missions and purposes and perpetuates itself" (Glazer, 1986, p. 7). Linked to the ritual of graduation, it is generally conferred with the imprimatur of an accredited institution's board of trustees, signifying completion of a program of study and marking the recipient's rite of passage into a higher level of academic endeavor or into the workforce. It originated in thirteenth-century European universities as a license to teach, and it soon became an obligation to teach. For two centuries, American higher education adhered to the British model, with the baccalaureate as the only earned degree following completion of a classical course of study (Storr, 1953). The master's degree was generally awarded *in cursu* to holders of the bachelor of arts who paid fees for three years following its completion. American universities had already adopted the European tradition of conferring honorary degrees at commencements and convocations. The first honorary degrees were granted by Harvard University—a Doctor of Sacred Theology conferred upon its president, Increase Mather, in 1692, and an honorary Master of Arts upon Benjamin Franklin in 1753 for "his great improvements in Philosophic Learning, particularly with respect to Electricity" (Freedman, 2003, p. 117). Two months later, in September 1753, Franklin was awarded a second honorary M.A. from Yale University. In 1851, Henry Tappan, president of the University of Michigan, originated a new prototype for American higher education, combining elements of English and German academic institutions (Spurr, 1970) and instituting the Master of Arts and Master of Science as earned degrees paralleling the undergraduate baccalaureate and the research doctorate (Ph.D.). Michigan conferred the nation's first earned M.A. in 1859. Identified as *secundum gradum in artibus,* the second degree in arts, it was essentially a liberal arts degree rather than a professional or discipline-based degree.

The earned M.A. and M.S. flourished in the late nineteenth and twentieth centuries as the first year of graduate school, partly because of the advent of coeducation, the emergence of the undergraduate core or general education curriculum, and the introduction of advanced courses beyond the baccalaureate in academic subjects (Storr, 1953). For those aspiring to teach in expanding postsecondary systems, however, the Ph.D. rather than the master's degree became the degree of choice. The reverse occurred in professional fields that emerged as parallel programs that would assure employment in such occupations as accounting, law, journalism, social work, and public school teaching. It was not until the mid-twentieth century that preparation in these fields combined preprofessional (baccalaureate) and professional development (master's) degrees.

The expansion of doctoral education in academic disciplines paralleled the growth of the research university from the 1880s through the 1960s. In his history of the research university, Geiger (1986) observes that in the late nineteenth century the "basic academic disciplines in the arts and sciences were organized into their current associations [and that] these groupings were merely formal manifestations of a more fundamental process of professionalization" characterized by the specialization of disciplinary knowledge, the social organization of membership in professional associations, meetings, and professional journals, and the university as the locus for practice of the disciplines (p. 20).

The founding of the Johns Hopkins University in 1876 as a graduate research university combining professional schools and doctoral research in one structure that was based on a continental model for advanced study became an influential model in the development of the American research university. Although the master's degree continued to be recognized as a viable credential for college faculty, by 1900 the newly established Association of American Universities (AAU), of which Johns Hopkins, Clark, Yale, and Harvard Universities were founding members, proclaimed the need for consolidation in the development of new graduate programs (Berelson, 1960; Spurr, 1970). The Ph.D. rather than the M.A. became the gold standard in the graduate degree hierarchy, growing in status and prestige and eclipsing the freestanding master's degree. Two parallel movements evolved as graduate education capped by the research doctorate became increasingly differentiated from the professional school.

In his excellent history of higher education, John Thelin (2004) describes the multidirectional shifts occurring in the late nineteenth and early twentieth centuries, the lack of consensus among academic leaders regarding support of the liberal arts and occupational-technical education, and the impact of public policy on its development. With federal funding, engineering emerged as a mainstay of the undergraduate curriculum at the two military academies, West Point and Annapolis. The Morrill Act of 1862 also spurred the growth of practical programs in engineering as well as agriculture, mining, and other technical fields. Teacher training benefited from the establishment of normal schools and women's seminaries, and by 1845 the New York State board of regents had authorized 145 normal schools and seminaries

(p. 79). By 1910, says Thelin, universities offered "a linear array of fields." In addition to the liberal arts baccalaureate and degrees in medicine and law, students could opt for "new professions," business, engineering, forestry, home economics, social work, and agriculture, a veritable "smorgasbord" of degrees as the heart of advanced studies (p. 153).

A Century of Reform

Inevitably, educational critics expressed their concern about the evolving pattern of differentiation in the academy. The AAU commissioned the first major study of the master's degree in 1909 to define its purpose as a research degree, an enrichment degree, or a prerequisite for secondary school certification. It found little standardization of requirements or in the use of degree titles, with M.A., M.S., and M.Phil. being used interchangeably. The disparities extended to residence requirements, specializations, lack of articulation with under-graduate departments, and the use of correspondence and extension credits, all of which it deplored (Association of American Universities, 1910; Glazer, 1986). In its self-appointed role as arbiter of standards, AAU set forth recommended parameters for master's education in its member universities. Criticism of the quality of medical education also led the Carnegie Foundation for the Advancement of Teaching to recruit Abraham Flexner to conduct a vigorous study of the nation's 155 medical schools. His highly critical report, issued in 1910, gained wide public attention, encouraging philanthropic assistance for "research-oriented scientifically based academic medicine" and, over the long range, elevating medical faculty, clinical professorships, and teaching hospitals to a position of status and prestige within evolving research universities (Brown, 1979, p. 156; Bonner, 2002).

One unintended consequence of the promotion of higher academic standards was to foster an unending cycle of credentialism within graduate and professional schools. Incremental changes in credit hours, clinical experiences, and criteria for initial licensing and certification had the net impact of raising entry-level requirements to the master's degree in a number of professional fields, among them medicine, law, social work, librarianship, corporate management, and school administration. It also prompted the introduction of a new degree taxonomy: the first-professional degree.[3] By the mid-twentieth century, the diversity of the master's degree made it difficult for educators to define its meaning with any precision. In 1945, the AAU Committee on Graduate Work reiterated concern about degree proliferation, recommending that types of master's degrees adhere to only four designations: the M.A. or M.S. as research degrees and the M.A.T. and M.Ed. as teaching degrees, with qualifying phrases for "technical" degrees—for example, the M.S. in engineering (Association of American Universities, 1945, p. 124).

Federal Aid and Quality Control

The National Defense Education Act of 1957, enacted following the Russian launch of *Sputnik,* opened the floodgates of federal aid to education. Millions of dollars became available for curricular reform in science, mathematics, and technology and for related teacher training. The accelerated growth of graduate and professional education throughout the 1960s raised issues about academic quality, student access, and degree proliferation. The decline in prestige and status of the research master's degree envisioned by AAU members was a source of much hand-wringing within the educational establishment. The Association of Graduate Schools stated that the master's degree needed to be "rehabilitated, revitalized, resuscitated, redefined, and readjusted" (Glazer, 1986, p. 10). The former president of the Carnegie Foundation, Oliver Carmichael, citing the "deplorable state of the M.A.," proposed a three-year master's degree in a discipline for those preparing to teach community college or lower-division undergraduates in four-year colleges and universities (1961, p. 3). The American Council on Education formed the Committee on Academic Degrees in 1962 to investigate the proliferation of master's degrees in professional and academic fields. It proposed an arbitrary limit of fifty on the number of master's degree designations and the standardization of abbreviations, particularly in business, education, and engineering, to eliminate what it viewed as a potentially chaotic situation (Glazer, 1986). By then, however, 150 master's degree designations were in use, mainly technical or vocational, while the master's and the doctorate were becoming more professionalized (p. 8). An influential report by Stephen Spurr, then president of the University of Texas at Austin, was issued by the Carnegie Commission on Higher Education, a major engine of reform in the 1970s. Spurr proposed a one-year academic master's, a two-year professional master's, a three-year first-professional, and a four-year doctorate (Spurr, 1970). He also proposed an intermediate Master of Philosophy (M. Phil.) as a stepping-stone to the Ph.D. Criticism of the emphasis given to specialized research in doctoral programs and concern that undergraduate teaching in the liberal arts was being neglected led to support for a teaching doctorate in humanistic studies, the Doctor of Arts (Glazer, 1993).[4] Other issues swirled around the baccalaureate as a terminal degree or way station to the master's degree, the allocation of student aid for combined B.A./M.A. or B.S./M.S. programs, and the concept of a three-year baccalaureate (comparable to the British model). One deterrent to more flexible degrees was restrictions on aid to full-time undergraduates; thus, by the 1970s, the Carnegie Commission on Higher Education and other policymakers were proposing changes in state and federal regulations to permit financial assistance to part-time and graduate students.

New York State became one of the first states, in 1969, to undertake a comprehensive study of first-year graduate work. Its Division of Teacher Education and Academic Program Review examined curricula in six hundred of the twenty-one hundred master's programs in public and private universities, prompting the board of regents to declare a moratorium, not on the master's degree but on the development of all new doctoral programs, and to adopt new regulations for the registration of undergraduate and graduate programs (State Education Department, 1972). These regulations called for needs assessments for new programs, professionalization of programs "to guide personal and career decisions of students," institutional accountability for program outcomes, and establishment of a system for evaluating program quality (p. iii). The board of regents appointed a doctoral council of graduate school deans to ratify new state regulations for the review and reregistration of master's and doctoral programs in public and private universities. This unprecedented action by a state governing board signaled to graduate school faculty and deans that their programs would now be subject to external peer reviews. The oversight of master's degrees was subsumed under the doctoral reviews, and a moratorium was declared on the approval of new doctorates in a number of low-enrollment fields, for example, philosophy, German, and Slavic studies. Graduate programs that failed to meet state criteria for reregistration were given probationary status or suspended from further operation.

In 1973, the Council of Graduate Schools (CGS), as a leading proponent of graduate education in the liberal arts and sciences, joined with the Graduate Record Examination Board to identify dimensions of quality in doctoral programs. The Dimensions of Quality project concluded that self-studies and multidimensional frameworks should be employed to measure and assess the quality of graduate programs. An ad hoc task force appointed by CGS sought to apply the doctoral dimensions of quality at the master's level in the conviction that an optimal master's degree program consists of a "preplanned and coherent sequence of lectures, seminars, discussions, and independent studies or investigations, designed to give the student the opportunity to learn from original sources in the library, from studies conducted in the laboratory, through creative scholarship (whether research or professionally oriented) and through research or professional practice in the field" (Council of Graduate Schools, 1976, p. 4).[5] The task force report, released at a conference on the assessment of quality in master's programs (Commission on Higher Education, 1979), raised questions about the knowledge base of incoming master's students, the contradictory objectives of master's programs, the lack of consensus on what constitutes professional education, the problematic interschool and interdepartmental collaboration, and the potential for conflicts of interest among deans, trustees, and employers in determining reputational rankings of their own and colleagues' programs.

Professionalizing Graduate Education

Whereas *access* and *equal opportunity* had been the buzzwords of the 1960s and 1970s, since the mid-1980s the discourse has been dominated by calls for academic excellence, national standards, and quality assessments. A pivotal concern emerging from this discourse has been the professionalization of graduate education. Until this time, professional education focused not on the M.A. or M.S. in arts and sciences but on the master's or first-professional degree in a specialized field of professional practice. In this context, the norms of professional education differed from those of graduate school master's programs, which, as noted earlier, tended to be intermediate credentials en route to the doctorate. To gain greater insight into the meaning of the divergent paths of graduate and professional master's education, this section draws on the work of sociologists who have studied the professions and professionalization in specialized fields.

"The Professionalization of Everyone?" (Wilensky, 1964) sought to differentiate between occupations and professions, defining professional work as "based on systematic knowledge or doctrine acquired only through long prescribed training" and adhering to "professional norms" that dictate technical competence, standards of performance, and adherence to a service ideal (p. 138). So regarded, professionalization was a process for gaining control over training and admission to practice and for organizing self-regulating communities with high-quality standards and ethical codes of conduct. To offset what he saw as a trend toward professionalization in higher education, Bledstein (1976) proposed a "vertical vision of the culture of professionalism" by providing a context for values in which degrees serve a symbolic purpose in legitimizing the authority of middle-class Americans. "By screening students upon entrance, formalizing courses of study, publishing textbooks, standardizing examinations and awarding degrees, educators convinced the public that objective principles rather than subjective partisanship determined competence in America" (p. 124). In his construct, occupations and their subcultures gain recognition and status as professions and academic sciences with distinct theories and intellectual requirements, and the vertical structure of the university reflects the upward direction in which power, privilege, prestige, and money flow throughout the larger society (p. 126).

The 1970s were a decade of great ferment in the professions as civil rights and equity laws provided increased access and opportunity into male-dominated fields. While some sociologists continued to define teaching, nursing, and other historically feminized fields as minor, service, quasi- or semiprofessions in contrast to male-dominated fields of theology, medicine, law, and architecture, a more egalitarian critique challenged the stratification of the professions within structures of social inequality, in which "classic, older professions sought to control their markets and to gain a privileged position in the occupational and social hierarchies" (Larson, 1979, p. 136).

In his review of research on the professions, Eliot Freidson, a sociologist of medicine, adheres to the hierarchical perspective advanced by Wilensky and Bledstein. He proposes an ideal-typical model of professionalism in which power, prestige, exclusivity, and status devolve to those with access to expert knowledge and skills, who secure their positions through specialized accrediting and licensing. He observes that although all professions are experiencing "great changes in their composition, numbers, and political influence," the "professional arena continues to be characterized by quasi-monopolies over core services, often sustained by exclusive licensing" and high levels of autonomy (Freidson, 1994, p. 199).

Andrew Abbott's system of professions (2001) refined the hierarchical model, asserting that the most prestigious professionals (for example, in medicine) work as consultants rather than offering primary care and that, within the university, research as a purely professional activity occupies a higher status (and greater extrinsic rewards) than classroom teaching. His case study of his own Department of Sociology at the University of Chicago led him to acknowledge that crisply defined patterns of disciplinary knowledge had given way to "the chaos of disciplines" in which "professions are organized around abstract knowledge and tend to grant prestige only to those most closely associated with its organizing principles—those who exercise the profession's knowledge in its purest form" (p. 148).

Randall Collins, who characterized American higher education as a "credential society" (1979), differs with those who adhere to the belief that professionalism and professionalization operate independently of the marketplace. He views academic credentialing as an important market consideration, stating that the "credential market has its own dynamics, quite apart from whatever level of skills the education provides" (1990, p. 20). Thus, the occupational payoff of a given level of education responds to the supply of educational credentials rather than to the level of skills required, adding another layer of social organization to the occupational structure, one that is particularly important in shaping the social identity of occupations (p. 20).

Michael Burrage and his colleagues concur with Collins's argument, theorizing that "every profession involves a relationship of some kind between four actors"—the universities, the practitioners, the state, and those individuals or groups who use their services. In this construct, practicing professions are "obviously the key actors in their own development" through their ability to control access to and practice of their professions (Burrage, Jarausch, and Siegrist, 1990, p. 207). The inclusion of "users" of professional services creates a framework in which the users, whether they are fee-for-service clients, trade unions, corporations, or third-party payers, have a stake in determining the status and prestige of the profession, reifying the importance of the marketplace in professionalization.

Steven Brint (1994) further asserts that the ideal of social trustee professionalism that had characterized graduate education for much of the twentieth century and was "proclaimed with some regularity by the leaders of the professional associations, by political leaders tied to the professional stratum, and by university officials" has given way to the promotion of a second ideal of "expert professionalism" (p. 39). In accord with Collins's observations and Burrage's framework, Brint (1994) argues persuasively that emphasis has shifted from civic responsibility for the greatest number of people to "the instrumental effectiveness of specialized, historically grounded knowledge, but including comparatively little concern with collegial organization, ethical standards, or service to the public interest" (p. 37). This culture of expert professionalism manifests itself most convincingly in the master's degree and the aptly named first-professional degree, both of which are evolving as credentials of social and economic currency for their recipients.

The European Model of Professionalization

Tony Becher and Paul Trowler (2001), in their study of twelve disciplines in U.K. universities, assert that regardless of institutional diversification, the majority of British faculty in universities and former polytechnics maintain their unswerving allegiance to their academic departments, exhibiting the behavior of "academic tribes" protecting their professional and disciplinary "territories." In the European Union, efforts are forging ahead to break down faculty resistance to collaboration across departmental, institutional, and national borders in conjunction with the Bologna Declaration. Signed originally by the education ministers of twenty-nine European countries in

June 1999 and subsequently confirmed at the Prague Summit in 2001, participation has since expanded to forty nations (Spinelli, 2003). Under the aegis of the European University Association (EUA), which is acting as the coordinating body, its aim is to create a European higher education structure by 2010 with three major objectives: the adoption of a system of comparable baccalaureate and master's degrees incorporating a unified credit system, the promotion of student and faculty mobility and international standards for quality assurance, and, for the long range, increased competitiveness of European higher education in the world market. This intergovernmental agreement includes large and small countries as well as the states of Andorra, Liechtenstein, and the Vatican, which are not mainstream providers. According to its provisions, the undergraduate baccalaureate must be at least three years in duration, at which time a degree will be awarded that "must be relevant to the European labour market as an appropriate qualification" (Spinelli, 2003, p. 2). The second cycle, which can lead to a master's degree, is estimated at two years in duration. A recent modification added a third cycle covering all doctoral degrees, which are also available through completion of a second master's cycle qualification. Now being implemented as part of that agreement is a standard European credit-transfer system that students may use to earn degrees in virtually all disciplines, from the humanities and social sciences to law and medicine. Other tools in development include a diploma supplement and proposals for "an overarching European qualifications framework" (Froment, 2005, p. 1).

A survey of master's degrees in thirty-one European nations noted the "significant variety with regard to the duration and architecture of degrees" (Tauch, 2002, p. 7). Perhaps the greatest differentiation in addition to requisite credit hours for the baccalaureate and master's degrees occurs in determining qualifications for academic and professional programs. Whereas some countries make little or no distinction in nomenclature, others are introducing new professional master's, or in some cases, are granting access to holders of equivalent qualifications (but not baccalaureate degrees), providing "more bridges between the professional higher education sector and the universities" (p. 7).

In the United Kingdom, master's degrees earned *in cursu* or for research carried out independently have been converted into "taught" master's degrees that are more entrepreneurial and less research-oriented than the models they replace. In an effort to strengthen its position in the social sciences, the Centre for International Studies at the University of Cambridge is restructuring its master's degree in international studies, offering both one-year full-time and two-year part-time tracks to meet the needs of students interested in adding "an international dimension to their education before entering politics, business, or the professions" (Hill, 2005, p. 18). A research component is its other major priority, engaging program faculty with scholars throughout the university interested in international affairs, particularly in politics, history, law, and economics (p. 18).

In their survey of professional doctorates now being offered in U.K. universities, Tom Bourner and his colleagues found that the "taught" master's is more likely to be required for admission to the professional Ed.D., for example, than for the traditional Ph.D. (2001). As Peter Knight observes in *Masterclass* (1997), the U.K. and Australia are pursuing a similar trend in which the growth of coursework masters, estimated at 58 percent, "has been accompanied by a shift away from traditional academic and liberal arts subjects to professional studies" (p. 2). A major concern is whether national standards and quality assurance will have a negative impact on student diversity and on the quality of postgraduate programs (Thorne, 1997). The issues being raised in the United Kingdom exemplify the difficulties of coordinating postgraduate frameworks across national borders and institutional territories. Some observers speculate that market forces will, in the final analysis, determine the international portability of second-cycle master's degrees in professional subjects. In a special issue of the *Times Higher Education* supplement, *Bologna: A Dream to Reality,* Tessa Blackstone, vice chancellor of the University of Greenwich and a former minister of state for education and employment in the United Kingdom, expresses the ministerial position that the creation of a European higher education structure will not only increase mobility and job opportunities for students but also make British higher education more competitive in the world market (2005).[6]

Professional and graduate education took two divergent paths throughout the history of American higher education. By the close of the twentieth century, however, these paths had begun to converge as a result of market forces that brought the university much closer to the corporate world. These cultural shifts have a major impact on the master's degree in the liberal arts and sciences, which now borrow from the most successful professional curricular models in redefining the content and structure of their programs. The central role of professionalization in this process continues to be critical to our understanding of the changes now taking place as American and European universities vie for global status.

The Changing Demographics of Master's Students

Data from the National Postsecondary Student Aid Study (NPSAS), shown in Table 1, provide a demographic profile of master's students by gender, age, and marital or dependent status by selected enrollment and institutional characteristics. By 1999–2000, the most recent year for which these data are available, master's candidates were older, more diverse, and more likely to be employed than their predecessors in the 1980s (Choy and Geis, 2002). Their average age was 32.6 years, almost 22 percent were older than forty years of age, and the largest concentration (34 percent) was in the 25–29 age category. Almost half were married (46 percent), more than a third had dependents (37 percent), and 59 percent were female. In reviewing attendance patterns, unmarried students with no dependents made up the largest percentage of students attending full time or part time, while unmarried students with dependents (who are likely to be single parents) had the lowest rates of attendance for the master's degree.

The NPSAS survey also estimated that 55 percent of all master's students attend public institutions, 42 percent private, nonprofit institutions, and 3.5 percent primarily private, for-profit institutions, the majority of this latter group in M.B.A. programs (Choy and Geis, 2002). As might be expected, given tuition differentials between public and private universities, the average financial aid package at private research universities was $14,086, compared with $7,970 at private nondoctoral institutions and $6,561 at public nondoctoral institutions. Full-time students also received higher levels of aid than part-time master's students. Similarly, those who attended doctorate-granting institutions received larger amounts of aid than those at nondoctoral institutions. As a result, doctoral candidates were more likely to enroll full time

TABLE 1
Percentage Distribution of Master's Students by Gender, Age, and Marital or Dependent Status, 1999–2000

	Gender		Age					Average	No Dependents		With Dependents	
	Male	Female	Under 25	25–29	30–34	35–39	40+	Age	Unmarried	Married	Unmarried	Married
Total	40.9	59.1	15.5	33.9	17.7	11.2	21.7	32.6	44.4	18.7	9.9	27.0
Public	39.1	61.0	17.0	34.4	16.2	10.8	21.7	32.4	43.7	19.1	10.3	26.9
Noncoctorate Granting	30.9	69.1	10.0	34.6	17.6	12.6	25.3	33.7	36.4	19.4	11.2	33.0
Doctorate Granting	42.1	57.9	19.6	34.3	15.7	10.1	20.3	31.9	46.4	19.0	9.9	24.7
Private Not for Profit	42.8	57.2	13.8	33.9	19.2	11.7	21.5	32.7	45.5	18.1	9.4	27.0
Nondoctorate Granting	42.0	58.1	11.6	28.9	19.4	11.4	28.7	34.0	35.6	18.0	9.8	36.6
Doctorate Granting	43.2	56.8	14.8	36.1	19.0	11.8	18.3	32.1	50.0	18.1	9.3	22.7
Degree Type												
Business Administration (M.B.A.)	60.2	39.8	11.2	39.6	21.5	12.4	15.3	31.6	43.2	19.5	9.3	27.7
Education (any Master's)	23.8	76.2	10.3	31.8	17.1	12.8	28.1	34.2	34.9	19.7	11.4	34.1
Other Master's of Arts (M.A.)	40.4	59.6	21.2	34.9	14.7	9.7	19.5	31.8	51.8	20.2	9.5	18.5
Other Master's of Science (M.S.)	47.0	53.0	22.4	33.6	18.0	8.9	17.0	31.0	51.4	18.8	8.0	21.8
Other Master's Degrees	39.7	60.3	17.4	31.2	16.0	10.6	24.8	33.1	47.8	15.6	10.5	26.1
Attendance Pattern												
Full Time, Full Year	47.6	52.4	30.7	38.3	14.2	6.7	10.2	28.8	64.6	14.3	6.5	14.6
Full Time, Part Year	45.9	54.1	22.0	37.4	14.2	8.5	17.9	31.2	50.1	17.2	11.3	21.3
Part Time, Full Year	41.2	58.8	9.1	31.7	19.1	12.6	27.5	34.4	39.7	21.2	9.2	29.9
Part Time, Part Year	37.0	63.1	8.9	25.2	18.9	12.9	34.1	35.9	34.4	21.0	12.0	32.6

SOURCE: Choy and Geis (2002).

(54 percent versus 27 percent) and to enroll directly from the bachelor's degree (25 percent versus 20 percent). Given the cost implications for completing a master's degree, proposals by professional associations, accrediting agencies, and state governing boards to extend the number of credit hours and capstone requirements in professional fields ranging from business and engineering to teacher education encounter strong resistance from candidates for these degrees and their advocates.

The social profile of master's students demonstrates a high level of participation of women, people of color, and international students. Table 2 disaggregates data on master's degrees awarded by field, sex, and race or ethnicity for 2001–2002.

Women earning master's degrees reached parity with men in 1981 (50.3 percent); by 2002 (as shown in Table 2), they earned 58.7 percent. The highest proportion of women master's recipients are in professional programs: library science (81.8 percent), health professions (77.6 percent), education (76.4 percent), psychology (76.4 percent), public administration (74.4 percent), communications (65.4 percent), and accounting (55.5 percent). In comparison, men are more likely to earn master's degrees in engineering (72.2 percent), computer science (66.7 percent), business (59 percent), physical sciences (62.4), and mathematics (57.6 percent).

Table 2 also shows that by 2001–2002, when master's degree recipients are disaggregated by race, ethnicity, and citizenship status, whites accounted for 62.1 percent, African Americans for 7.7 percent, Hispanics for 4.2 percent, Asian/Pacific Islanders for 4.8 percent, and Native Americans for 0.5 percent. U.S. women were also granted the majority of master's degrees earned by African Americans (71 percent), Asians (54.2 percent), Hispanics (62.8 percent), and Native Americans (62.5 percent). In contrast, men constituted the majority of nonresident alien master's degree recipients (58.7 percent), reflecting their predominance in business, engineering, physical science, and mathematics.

It is clear from these data that non-U.S. citizens, particularly from Asian countries, are boosting enrollments for master's degrees. Because these students are not eligible for federal grant and loan programs, financial aid generally occurs through assistantships. In 2000, 54 percent received an assistantship, compared with 17 percent of U.S. citizens and resident aliens, a statistic that

TABLE 2

Master's Degrees Awarded by Field, Sex, and Race or Ethnicity, 2001–2002

Field	Total	Percent Women	Percent White	Percent African American	Percent Hispanic	Percent Asian	Percent Native American	Percent Nonresident Alien
All Fields	482,118	58.7	62.1	7.7	4.2	4.8	0.5	13.2
Agriculture and Natural Resources	4,519	48.1	72.8	2.5	2.4	2.9	0.6	9.7
Architecture	4,566	42.9	55.9	3.3	4.4	5.3	0.3	24.2
Area, Ethnic, and Cultural Studies	1,578	61.3	53.3	7.2	7.0	5.9	1.3	14.9
Biological Sciences	6,205	57.8	64.8	4.6	4.0	8.4	0.5	12.7
Business, Management, and Marketing	120,784	41.0	55.8	7.7	3.7	6.1	0.4	16.6
Communications and Communication Technologies	6,059	63.7	57.9	8.6	3.0	4.1	0.3	19.4
Computer and Information Sciences	16,113	33.3	27.6	4.0	1.6	12.1	0.2	47.3
Education	136,579	76.4	72.6	8.8	5.2	2.1	0.6	2.9
Engineering and Engineering Technologies	26,911	21.4	40.4	3.0	2.7	8.3	0.2	40.8
English Language/Literature	7,268	68.0	74.9	4.4	3.1	3.2	0.6	6.7
Foreign Languages/Literature	2,861	69.2	50.8	1.7	11.2	3.7	0.2	25.7

Health Professions and Related Sciences	43,644	77.6	70.9	7.0	3.7	7.1	0.5	4.8
Home Economics	2,608	85.1	68.7	9.7	4.7	3.7	0.8	6.9
Law and Legal Studies	4,053	41.8	25.7	3.5	3.3	4.1	0.2	53.9
Liberal Arts, General Studies, and Humanities	2,754	62.6	70.8	7.0	3.9	2.4	0.7	6.3
Library Science	5,113	81.8	78.1	4.7	3.9	2.8	0.6	3.5
Mathematics	3,487	42.4	45.8	3.4	2.3	6.3	0.3	37.3
Multi/Interdisciplinary Studies	3,211	61.5	63.1	7.1	4.4	4.2	0.7	12.3
Parks, Recreation, Leisure, and Fitness	2,754	50.7	77.6	7.3	2.5	2.0	0.3	6.4
Philosophy and Religion	1,334	37.8	72.4	4.0	2.5	4.3	0.3	8.0
Physical Sciences	5,009	37.6	57.0	2.8	2.8	5.0	0.4	27.8
Protective Services	2,935	45.0	65.1	14.9	4.9	1.8	0.8	3.1
Psychology	14,888	76.4	67.9	11.4	5.7	3.7	0.7	3.3
Public Administration, Policy, Social Work	25,448	74.4	62.4	16.2	6.4	3.3	0.8	5.2
Social Sciences and History	14,112	50.8	56.5	6.7	4.4	3.7	0.5	22.0
Theological Studies	4,952	38.1	68.5	6.4	3.2	5.3	0.2	12.1
Transportation	709	10.7	79.0	4.2	4.1	1.4	0.4	3.9
Visual and Performing Arts	11,595	57.6	62.2	4.0	3.4	4.5	0.4	18.2
Not Classified	69	39.1	60.9	4.3	5.8	4.3	0.0	24.6

SOURCE: Data derived from National Center for Education Statistics, *Postsecondary Institutions in the United States: Fall 2002 and Degrees Conferred, 2001–02*; and Commission on Professionals in Science and Technology, Table M3 06, retrieved March 1, 2005, from http://www.sciencesmasters.org.

reflects to some extent their enrollment in science and engineering programs where funding is more readily available through faculty research grants. Aggressive marketing strategies that had been used to recruit international students have been hampered since September 11, 2001, as a result of tighter visa and security regulations following the attacks on the World Trade Center.

The flow of students is also being restricted as a result of greater competition from other English-speaking countries, a phenomenon that is predicted to accelerate by 2010 as an outcome of the formalized cooperation agreements among European higher education institutions. In a CGS survey, 113 graduate deans reported one-year average declines of 28 percent in 2003–2004 international graduate student applications. The greatest losses were in engineering and the sciences, but declines were also reported in agriculture, business, education, humanities, and social sciences (Syverson, 2004). Subsequent surveys by CGS revealed an average 18 percent decrease in international admissions offers and a 6 percent decrease in international first-time graduate enrollment. A joint survey conducted in fall 2004 by five higher and international education associations reported a continuing decline among schools with sizable commitments to foreign students, particularly in enrollments of new engineering and business graduate students (Association of International Educators, 2004). President Hasselmo of the AAU attributes these declines to U.S. visa policy, increased international competition, and perceptions that the United States "is no longer a welcoming country" (Association of American Universities, 2004). Underlying concerns of American universities are economic imperatives that help sustain the graduate enterprise. The potential loss of revenue from a precipitous decline in international students cannot but have a serious impact on graduate, including master's, programs among universities that are major importers, particularly in business, engineering, and the sciences.

Curricular Models of Master's Education

A S A PIVOTAL DEGREE THAT BRIDGES THE BACCALAUREATE, THE DOCTORATE, AND THE WORKPLACE, the master's degree has the capacity to continually evolve as a highly adaptable and affordable credential. Its significance in the degree hierarchy is also linked to the development of new organizational structures that increasingly characterize the work of the university—offices of technology transfer, industrial liaison, research networks, consortia, and entrepreneurial firms where "research is typically problem-focused and often collaborative at the interfaces of disciplines" (Klein, 2000, p. 5). These arrangements have significant implications for understanding the evolution of graduate education from hierarchical, bounded disciplines into heterogeneous organizational frameworks that superimpose interdisciplinarity as an overarching system of innovation, boundary crossing, and interaction among scientific, technological, and industrial modes of knowledge production (Nowotny, Scott, and Gibbons, 2001). They resonate with recommendations of public and private agencies for the preparation of graduate students in an interdisciplinary and global job market and with students seeking favorable economic returns on their educational investment.

Sociologists of knowledge assert that the production of basic and applied knowledge is no longer primarily disciplinary but exhibits interactive characteristics, described as "a constant flow back and forth between the fundamental and the applied, between the theoretical and the practical" (Gibbons and others, 1994, p. 19). In this phase (referred to by Gibbons as "Mode 2"), knowledge production is oriented toward contextualized results that engage faculty and practitioners from different disciplines and backgrounds, working collaboratively in a "proliferation of sites outside normal disciplinary structures and institutions" (p. 22). Although their findings have not been construed in terms of academic degrees, the fields they cite as exemplars—biotechnology, information technology, microelectronics, and artificial intelligence—illustrate the shift from basic to applied fields that gain in prestige and purpose through inter- or multidisciplinary practice (p. 24).

In developing a conceptual vocabulary for studying curriculum diversification and interdisciplinarity, Julie Klein (1993) applies Clifford Geertz's metaphor of blurred genres to describe the "growing number of cross-disciplinary borrowings, projects, and new categories of knowledge that document increased permeation of disciplinary boundaries" (p. 187). In his earlier ruminations on knowledge construction, Geertz (1983) had interrogated "grand rubrics like 'Natural Science,' 'Biological Science,' 'Social Science,' and 'The Humanities'" as artifices used to organize curricula, sort scholars into cliques and professional communities, and distinguish broad traditions of intellectual style (p. 7). Nevertheless, he argued, problems arise in assuming that these rubrics are "borders-and-territories map(s) of modern intellectual life, or, worse, a Linnaean catalogue into which to classify scholarly species" (p. 7). Klein (2000) extends that argument, citing the importance of applying explanatory frameworks that advance practical and scholarly understanding of inter- and multidisciplinarity, rejecting adherence to traditional spatial metaphors of turf, territory, boundary, and domain and the territorial claims and expansionist strategies that characterize them. Earlier, she cited four kinds of interaction that constitute interdisciplinarity in actual practice: borrowing (of analytical tools, disciplinary methods, and conceptual frameworks), solving problems, the emergence of interdisciplines, and the increased consistency of subject matters and methods, thereby creating such "new" disciplines as psycholinguistics, biophysics, and biochemistry (Klein, 1990, p. 64). Beyond the sciences, changes in the content and context of master's education in the social, behavioral, and natural sciences foreshadow a professionalized mission for graduate education, one that is more concerned with applied knowledge, cultural interpretations, and social accountability.

A valuable source of demographic and trend data on graduate degree recipients is derived from the Survey of Earned Doctorates conducted annually by the National Opinion Research Center (NORC) at the University of Chicago (Hoffer and others, 2003). The statistical profile of doctorate recipients shows that in 2003, 52 percent had completed the bachelor's degree in the same field as their Ph.D., while 73 percent had completed a master's degree in any field (Hoffer and others, 2003, p. 108). As shown in Table 3, the highest percentage of doctoral recipients who obtained master's degrees in *any* field of study were in education (85.8 percent), humanities (83.5 percent), and engineering (82.5 percent). Education doctorate recipients were also most likely to have earned baccalaureates (and possibly master's degrees) in master's colleges and universities. Doctorate holders in physical sciences (60.7 percent) and life sciences (52.3 percent) were less likely to have completed a master's en route to the Ph.D. In contrast, doctoral recipients in the sciences were more likely than in the humanities and social sciences to have completed a baccalaureate in the

TABLE 3
Statistical Profile of Doctorate Recipients: Master's and Baccalaureate Data, 2002–2003

Field	Percentage of Ph.D.s with Master's Degree in Any Field	Percentage of Ph.D.s with Baccalaureate in Same Field
2003 Total	72.9	52.4
Education	85.8	31.0
Engineering	82.5	74.4
Humanities	83.5	60.2
Life Sciences	52.3	47.8
Physical Sciences	60.7	65.3
Social Sciences	77.3	52.2
Professional and Other Fields*	81.7	28.4

SOURCE: *Doctorate Recipients from United States Universities: Summary Report 2003*, pp. 108, 109. The Survey of Earned Doctorates is sponsored by the National Science Foundation, the National Institutes of Health, the U.S. Department of Education, the National Endowment for the Humanities, the U.S. Department of Agriculture, and the National Aeronautics and Space Administration. It provides a statistical profile of doctorate recipients by major field of study, gender, race, ethnicity, and citizenship status. This table disaggregates data on the percentage of doctorates who obtained a master's degree in *any* field of study en route to the doctorate and the percentage of doctorates who completed the baccalaureate in the *same* field as their Ph.D. (Hoffer and others, 2003).
NOTE: *"Professional and other fields" refers to two large-enrollment fields: business and management, and communications, and ten smaller fields, including architecture, library sciences, public administration, social work, and theology (Hoffer and others, 2003, p. 152).

same field as their doctorate. Education, business, and other professional doctorate recipients were much less likely to have done undergraduate work in their field, not surprising given the fact that professional fields are predominantly taught at the graduate level. The Survey of Earned Doctorates also reports that between 1999 and 2003, 62 percent of all doctorate recipients earned baccalaureates from doctoral and research universities, compared with 21 percent at master's colleges and universities. The highest percentage of doctorates who completed undergraduate degrees in master's institutions were in education (34.4 percent) and professional fields (25 percent) (Hoffer and others, 2003, p. 80).

Degree Diversity and Disciplinary Taxonomies

The Survey of Earned Doctorates uses a classification system developed by the National Science Foundation. It is not the only system being used to facilitate the collection and presentation of statistical data on enrollments, degrees, staffing, facilities, and resources. Over the years, various taxonomies have been systematized to facilitate quantitative data analyses on a range of topics and issues. The growth of interdisciplinarity, the emergence of online education, and the production of new knowledge reveal the limitations of existing constructs. Although operational categories provide convenient sorting mechanisms for data collection and reporting purposes, institutions may also devise typologies that categorize master's degrees as basic or advanced, research or practitioner, intermediate or terminal, general or specialized, preprofessional or professional, fast-track or multiyear, online or on campus, dual or combined.

Admissions requirements may include standardized test scores such as the Graduate Record Examination, undergraduate prerequisites and grade point averages, work experience, and provisional certification in specialized fields, for example, in nursing and teacher education. The professional master's degree prominent among current offerings tends to be freestanding and inter- or multidisciplinary with an emphasis on core and applied knowledge, technological and communication skills, and the completion of field-based internships, problem-solving practica, and research projects in lieu of research theses. Fast-track versions of the professional master's program may also incorporate online and distance education components (or, in a growing number of institutions, be offered entirely online). The academic master's degree, on the other hand, may constitute the first year of predoctoral coursework and comprise core courses, elective cognates, a thesis or project, and a comprehensive examination. The academic and professional master's degrees anchor two ends of a continuum that represents the growing diversity of contemporary master's degree programs.

In 2004, Snyder, Tan, and Hoffman reported data on twenty-nine fields and 426 subfields, the highest being in education (fifty-six), health professions (forty-one), agriculture and natural resources (thirty-six), and business (thirty-one). In the humanities and sciences, the number ranged from five in mathematics and nine in English to twenty-one in physical sciences and twenty-five in life sciences. This expansion of master's degrees by field has led some critics to suggest that overproduction is having a negative impact on the meaning of graduate education. Others view it as an inevitable consequence of the reconfiguration of knowledge "through a 'specialization-fragmentation-hybridization' process whereby knowledge units merge and develop into various informal and institutionalized structures" (Dogan and Pahre, 1990, cited in Palmer, 2001, p. 8). In her cogent analysis of boundary crossing in the interdisciplinary research process, Palmer uses the example of psychology to describe the reconfiguration process, defining it as a "conglomeration of hybrids that includes social psychology, physiological psychology, political psychology, behavioral pharmacology, and cognitive science. In particular, cognitive science, which draws from linguistics, computer science, neuroscience, and philosophy, illustrates psychology's interconnections with outside fields" (Palmer, 2001, p. 8).

The National Research Council (NRC), which conducted two assessments of research doctoral programs in 1982 and 1993, is responding to these shifts in disciplinary configuration with proposals to restructure its taxonomy of academic fields and subfields. Its Panel on Taxonomy and Interdisciplinarity now recommends disaggregating data into fifty-seven fields of study—an increase from forty-one fields in the 1995 taxonomy—in four major areas: life sciences; physical sciences, mathematics, and engineering; arts and humanities; and social and behavioral sciences (National Research Council, 2003, pp. 21, 22). Subsumed within these fields are ninety-nine subfields ranging from bioinformatics to Indo-European linguistics and philology. Significantly for professional schools, the panel has decided *not* to include fields for which research is primarily directed to the improvement of practice, for example, social work, public policy, nursing, public health, business, architecture, criminology, and education (National Research Council, 2003, p. 20), but it has determined that agricultural sciences, biomedical sciences in medical schools, and communication should be added to the list of fields being surveyed.

The challenges encountered by the NRC panel in devising the new taxonomy (whose adoption has been delayed since 2003) substantiate the complexity of curricular transformation in graduate education, the "frequent disparity among institutional nomenclatures, representing essentially the same research and training activities, . . . the rise of interdisciplinary work" (p. 19), and the difficulties inherent in efforts to distinguish between disciplinarity and interdisciplinarity in many graduate programs—particularly when degrees that are conferred by discipline are taught by faculty who may also conduct their research in multiple disciplines or through centers and institutes. Or the placement of these programs may vary from one institution to another, depending on faculty interest and school of origin. For example, in some universities, film studies may be housed in the English department and in others in the visual and performing arts. In this context, the panel acknowledges the need not only to reorganize existing fields but also to add ten emerging fields, which are gaining impetus at the master's level, to its taxonomy: biotechnology; systems biology; nanoscience and nanotechnology; information science; science and technology studies; film studies; feminist, gender, and sexuality studies; and race, ethnicity, and postcolonial studies.

NCES subsumes these emerging fields into disciplinary categories, disaggregating only a limited number of degrees as "multi/interdisciplinary studies." The prolonged deliberations of the NRC panel indicate the complexities of disciplinary classification systems at the pinnacle of degree hierarchies. Although it is beyond the scope of this study to critique the practice of ranking graduate and professional schools and their departments, the ramifications of doing so in terms of institutional status and prestige are carefully scrutinized at the highest levels of academia. Less rigorous rankings than the NRC survey compiled by *U.S. News & World Report, Business Week, Financial Times,* and *Change,* among others, provide annual box scores for weighing the prominence or visibility of individual programs and are widely used in institutional marketing to recruit students and faculty and to generate external grants and contracts.

Professional associations continue to express their concern that the growth of degree designations will further stratify their professions by assigning different levels of status and prestige. Institutions have been undeterred, however, in their quest for financial stability as well as for national and international prominence. The blurred genres that Geertz and Klein describe are exemplified in the plethora of degree types and titles. In 1985, for example, Peterson's guide to graduate programs listed fifty professional doctorate titles, 667 master's degree titles, and 639 abbreviations; by 2005, those numbers had escalated to eighty-nine professional doctorate titles, more than one thousand master's degree titles, and nine hundred master's degree abbreviations (Peterson's, 2005, pp. 2357–2373)—not only the well-established M.A. and M.S. degrees but also more specialized degrees in areas such as electronic commerce, electro-optics, intellectual property, pest management, and clinical epidemiology. Combined degree programs are predominantly pairings with the M.B.A. or the J.D., each of which may be taken concurrently with a master's degree in education, science, public policy, social welfare, and (increasingly) other fields. Additional post-J.D. master's degrees in legal specialties include labor relations, tax, international, maritime, and public interest law. And in medicine, M.D. recipients may take master's degrees in clinical research or in public health, including specializations in aerospace, occupational, and preventive medicine (either the M.P.H. or the M.S.P.H.). The impact of technology on degree diversity pervades a number of disciplines. In library science, for example, the conventional Master of Library Science (M.L.S.) is one option; others include the Master of Library and Information Science (M.L.I.S.), the Master of Science in Information Studies (M.S.I.S.), the online M.S./L.I.S. with a specialization in the management of digital information (M.D.I.), and the M.A. or M.S. in Archival Studies. The American Association of Library Schools has also transformed itself into the Association of Library and Information Science Education, an organization of fifty-six schools and departments that offer library and information science master's degrees accredited by the American Library Association. Thirty-four of these schools offer post-master's degrees or certificates in advanced specializations. Thirty-two offer ninety joint degrees, mainly in history, law, business, English, music, and library science and information studies (Daniel and Saye, 2003). A joint master's degree in library science and information studies and a liberal arts or professional field is the preferred model for academic librarians who are expected to be specialists in one or more disciplines.

Alternative Delivery Systems

Nowhere is entrepreneurship more apparent than in schools of continuing education and professional studies and their complementary ventures into distance education and online learning. The growing investment in alternative delivery systems for educating large numbers of students on a global scale and with little regulation is creating new markets for master's education and greater profits for their institutions.

Continuing Education and Professional Studies

Master's degrees traditionally have been offered through graduate and professional schools of colleges and universities. In the 1970s, however, universities recognized that nontraditional adult students residing in their local communities constituted an untapped market for continuing and professional education. Operating outside the restrictions of faculty curriculum committees, accrediting agencies, and state boards, continuing education offered personal enrichment and noncredit courses proposed and taught by part-time adjunct faculty and scheduled at extension centers or branch campuses outside the regular school day, and increased use of the physical plant during less busy evenings, summers, and weekends. University Without Walls, Empire State College in New York, Fielding Institute, Western Governors University, and other external degree institutions provide further options for students seeking individualized and independent study. This movement is being institutionalized as universities reach out to business and government for new sources of students and external partnerships. By the 1990s, fast-track, online, and on-site master's degree programs had assumed a larger role in academic planning. At New York University, for example, students in the School of Professional and Continuing Studies may

choose from eleven M.S. degrees, two of which are offered through its Virtual College, which combines on-site and online sessions leading to degrees in instructional design or management and systems. Other M.S. degrees are offered in marketing, real estate, travel and tourism, publishing, and global studies.

Online Education

The virtual university that offers online degrees is a growing phenomenon. An online survey of chief academic officers at 1,170 institutions conducted by the Sloan Consortium and the Sloan Center for OnLine Education found that in 2003, 1.9 million students enrolled in online courses and that administrators predicted enrollments would reach 2.6 million by 2004 (Allen and Seaman, 2004). Not surprisingly, for-profit colleges dominate this market, anticipating a 40 percent enrollment increase in online courses, "almost double the rate among public or private nonprofit universities and colleges" (p. 9). Virtually every public university offers online education; their administrators are more likely than those at private institutions to assert that online learning is an essential strategy. The University of Massachusetts, which founded UMassOnline at its Boston campus in 2001, now admits students to any of its five degree-granting campuses for online bachelor or master's degrees in the liberal arts and professional disciplines (Flaherty, 2004). The University of Connecticut offers the thirty-six-credit master of professional studies (M.P.S.) as an online degree in four applied fields: homeland security leadership, human resource management, humanitarian services administration, and occupational safety and health management. It is available to students "anywhere in the world and at a time that fits into each student's schedule" for completion within two years (College of Continuing Studies, 2005). ClassesUSA, a Web site directory, lists fifty-five cyberspace providers whose distance learning programs are structured mainly for graduate and professional students. Online degrees offered by satellite and on the Internet include the M.B.A. and M.S. degrees in computer engineering, environmental systems management, microelectronics, health care administration, and e-education. Inevitably, a thirty-six-credit professional Master of Distance Education (M.D.E.) degree is now offered jointly by the University of Maryland University College and the University of Oldenburg (Germany), both leaders in distance education (Rubin, Bernath, and

Parker, 2004). Started in 2000, the M.D.E. enrolls three hundred students from 38 states and 12 nations. Maryland's University College originated as an adult education school and now offers seventeen master's degrees, all of which are available online, in business, management, technology, and education. The University of Oldenburg is a leader in distance education in Germany and in the development of asynchronous learning networks (p. 5).

Reframing Master's Education

Two recent studies propose categories of master's degrees that both extend and ignore federal taxonomies—the "positioned subject" model designed by Conrad, Haworth, and Millar (1993) and the "classical-applied-professional-hybrid" model designed by Syverson and Sims (2003). The positioned subject model is based on forty-seven case studies of master's programs in eleven fields at thirty-seven universities. Stakeholders in this multicase study were drawn from the ranks of administrators, faculty, students, alumni, and employers of program graduates. The study included professional and liberal arts fields and codified data from 781 interviews into five types of decision-situations and four program models. Interview data were organized by program orientation, modes of teaching and learning, and levels of institutional and departmental support. Four program types were derived: apprenticeship (participatory, skills centered, and professionally oriented); community centered (experiential, interdisciplinary, project and practice oriented); career advancement (reliance on core and specialized courses, theory-into-practice pedagogy, flexible scheduling, and faculty practitioners); and ancillary (predoctoral, research oriented, specialized theoretical knowledge, and critical understanding of methodologies and program content).

The positioned subject model again illustrates the complexity and diversity of master's education. The subjectivity of stakeholders in assessing program outcomes and the professionalization of master's education across and between disciplines raise unresolved issues regarding ideal-typical models. In this multicase study, disciplines and specializations are often categorized in more than one type, depending on the institution where they are housed. As a result, three case studies of English place it in three distinct categories based on stakeholders' responses. A community-centered M.A. in English is viewed as "client-centered, career-oriented, expert training" (Conrad, Haworth, and Millar, 1993, p. 178), an ancillary model at a research university is perceived as having "little cachet in the job market" (p. 142), and a six-week summer course in creative writing at a predominantly black institution is viewed as an "inexpensive and convenient way" to obtain content and skills en route to earning credentials for high school or community college teaching (p. 178). The vitality of these programs, according to interviewees, underscores the multiple meanings of an M.A. in English, contextualized around different missions, faculty, and students. It also illustrates the extent of faculty resistance to cross-disciplinary work, reinforced by like-minded attitudes and values of colleagues in professional societies. As Conrad, Haworth, and Millar clearly demonstrate, these values can and do determine the structure, content, and outcomes of the degree hierarchy and, to a large extent, whether the master's is construed as predoctoral coursework, summer enrichment, or a terminal degree. Other factors appear to be linked to accreditation or certification standards imposed externally by professional societies, state governing boards, and accrediting agencies. More serendipitous distinctions demonstrate the problems of typologies, that is, the self-interest of stakeholders as "positioned subjects" and how well their voices resonate in the disciplinary discourse. This model, however, provides insights on how students and faculty in particular value their education. To call the master's degree "a silent success" as the authors do in the title of their study, however ironically, may miscalculate the embeddedness of this degree in the fabric of graduate and professional education.

A different model proposed by the Council of Graduate Schools was derived from a multistage sampling process designed by Syverson and Sims (2003). A modified version of their classification matrix is contained in Borchert and Sims (2005, p. 6). Its purpose was to identify those variables or indicators that most closely defined the professional social science degree. Web site analyses were conducted of 350 programs in seventy graduate schools with varying rates of degree productivity and a clear focus on master's education. In grouping their professional indicators into four attributes of master's programs—number and type of skills-based courses, requisite internships and related activities, outcomes assessment, and employer advisory board participation—they highlighted the professional character of disciplinary clusters. Based on their research, they divided ten fields into three clusters: history and linguistics; sociology, geography, anthropology, and political science; and economics, communications, and psychology. This study revealed that private universities were more likely than public ones to display indicators of professionalization, particularly in public administration, anthropology, economics, sociology, and psychology; however, the reverse was true for programs in geography, history, linguistics, and political science. And significantly in relation to institutional classification systems, master's programs in all fields at doctoral universities incorporated more frequently exhibited professional characteristics than programs at master's universities, with the exception of programs in linguistics and sociology. Four categories were proposed: classical (predoctoral and programs grounded in theoretical and research methodologies); applied (focused on a specific area of practice with little direct relationship to prospective employers); professional (interdepartmental, community centered, and employment oriented); and hybrid (combining elements of two of the dominant program types). The attempt by Syverson and Sims to rationalize programs based on a self-imposed set of indicators underscores the difficulty of using objective measures across a diverse array of programs and institutions. They hypothesize, based on their preliminary research, that globalization, privatization, accountability mandates, and demographic changes in the social composition of graduate students may provide the impetus for professionalization of the social sciences.

Curricular models of higher education have diverged dramatically from the original concept of the American master's degree granted *in cursu* to recognize the efforts of those students who spend an additional year of study in their baccalaureate field under the guidance of a master teacher (Spurr, 1970). The multiple meanings of master's education have made it difficult to define except in rather basic arbitrary terms. As Conrad, Haworth, and Millar (1993) demonstrate, numerous factors either impede or facilitate teaching and learning across virtually every discipline or interdiscipline. The number and diversity of degree titles and taxonomies challenge state and federal efforts to quantify or standardize master's education. And as indicated in analyses of the construction of knowledge, the lines between basic and applied research and between disciplines and broad fields are changing rapidly.

Major Professional Programs

A T THE MASTER'S LEVEL, PROFESSIONAL SCHOOLS PRE-
DOMINATE in the constellation of colleges and universities, having long
since overtaken the arts and sciences as terminal credentials that connect more
directly with the workplace. Figure 1 compares master's degrees in selected fields
for over two decades from 1980–1981 through 2001–2002, the most recent
year for which master's degree data are reported by NCES.

It reveals the persistence of a disproportionate share in education (28 percent)
and business (25 percent), a total of 53 percent of all master's degrees awarded
in 2001–2002, compared with 49 percent in 1990–1991 and 52 percent in
1980–1981. Two other professional fields shown in this figure have experienced
significant increases: engineering has more than doubled from 5.6 percent of market share in 1980–1981 to 11 percent in 2001–2002, and health professions,
which include nursing, rehabilitation services, and medical-related master's
degrees, also show a steady climb from 5.6 percent to 9.1 percent by 2001–2002.
In contrast, the core fields of the university, liberal arts and sciences, show declines
in the proportion of master's degrees awarded. The sciences (which combine biological and physical science) account for only 2.3 percent of the total in
2001–2002, the social sciences (including psychology and history) for 6 percent,
and the humanities (including English and foreign languages and literature, and
philosophy) for 2.4 percent. In regard to student choice at the master's level, these
data highlight the growth of support for professional master's programs and the
proportionate decline of participation in established academic fields. Although
the student choice literature has tended to focus on the baccalaureate rather
than the master's degree, several reasons can be given for this trend.

FIGURE 1
Master's Degrees in Selected Fields, 1980–1981, 1990–1991, and 2000–2001

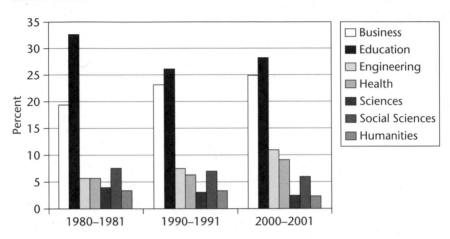

As universities have made the bachelor's degree a prerequisite for admission to professional schools, the master's and first-professional degrees have gained in status and prestige. Faculty trained in the professions have been ardent proponents for the further professionalization of their specialties. Accreditation, licensure, and certification provide the requisite mechanisms, reflecting the gatekeeping role of professional associations and state and federal regulatory agencies. Affirmative action laws and regulations encourage formerly single-sex universities and professional schools to admit women and minority students into the status fields of business, law, architecture, and medicine. Professional schools have transformed themselves into centers for the production of professionally relevant knowledge and its applications in professional practice. Their alliance with professional and accrediting agencies has led to the adoption of externally developed criteria for assessment and evaluation of their facilities, staff, and curricula, and concurrence on appropriate standards for accreditation and licensure.

Two fields that have been prominent in this context and that produce more than half of all master's degrees are business and education. They also prove the exception to the rule that the B.A.–M.A. trajectory is part of a continuum from basic to advanced study before entering the workforce. Approximately two-thirds of M.B.A. candidates have worked for an average of three years before enrolling in business schools, and 87 percent continue to work while enrolled, 75 percent of them full time (Choy and Geis, 2002). Fast-track and executive M.B.A. programs for those with work experience and undergraduate degrees in business also vie with extended two- to three-year professional M.B.A.s that encompass one or more specializations. An even larger proportion of education master's students (91 percent) remain in the workforce while studying for their degrees. Many of these students are already teaching and return to graduate schools to meet state or local district requirements, to qualify for salary increments, or to obtain certification and training in an allied teaching field. In education, the lines are increasingly blurred between pre-professional and professional degree programs. Some states mandate the elimination of undergraduate education degrees (Colorado and California, for example), while others now require students to complete field placements in each specialization for which they are seeking certification (New York, for example). Thus, the elementary school teacher who enrolls in a master's program in secondary special education and English in a New York state school of education may now be required to complete additional student teaching placements in special education and English at the middle and high school levels to qualify for state certification.

Business

The M.B.A. is an American invention and one of higher education's most successful exports. It originated in 1881 with the founding of the Wharton School at the University of Pennsylvania. The Harvard Business School, established in 1908, was the first of its kind to require a university degree for entry into a graduate M.B.A. program; it awarded its first degrees in 1910. Throughout the 1950s, schools of business and management proliferated, but in 1959 two reports funded by the Ford and Carnegie Foundations (Gordon and Howell, 1959; Pierson, 1959) took issue with their vocationalism and mediocrity. Subsequent efforts to limit production of undergraduate business degrees and make the M.B.A. the entry-level degree led to greater quality control, quantitatively rigorous coursework, less commercial specialization in undergraduate education, and the development of the business doctorate. Rather than stemming the production of business graduates, however, it accelerated the development of new M.B.A. specializations within existing business schools and the establishment of graduate business programs in liberal arts colleges, in master's-granting universities, and, most recently, among distance education providers in the United States, Europe, Asia, and Australia. The M.B.A. is undeniably the degree of choice for those seeking higher salaries and access to multinational corporations, investment banks, and entrepreneurial firms.

More than 60 percent of baccalaureates in business pursue the M.B.A. or other business degrees in approximately thirteen hundred universities, business schools, and management colleges in 126 countries worldwide. The global presence of these schools is evident in the widespread adoption of the M.B.A. by online and for-profit enterprises. The Association to Advance Collegiate Schools of Business (AACSB International) was founded in 1916 at a meeting of twenty-one representatives from seventeen universities with schools or programs in business. By 1919, it had adopted accreditation standards that now recognize 427 accredited programs, the majority of which (85 percent) are both undergraduate and graduate. AACSB member schools total 913: of that number, 655 are in the United States, 212 are outside the United States, and forty-six are corporate, government, and nonprofit institutions (Association to Advance Collegiate Schools of Business, 2004). By 1991, AACSB changed its criteria for accreditation, shifting the emphasis from input measures (data on faculty, students, facilities, and resources) to outcome measures "that monitor achievement of program objectives" and "promote continuous quality improvement" (Palomba and Palomba, 1999, p. 4). As in other professional fields, AACSB-accredited business schools are expected to systematically monitor M.B.A. programs, assessing their effectiveness in terms of student achievement, job placement, and feedback from alumni and employers. To familiarize faculty and deans with assessment criteria and techniques, AACSB also conducts an annual continuous improvement symposium.

A set of more rigorous standards approved in 2003 and applicable to business programs globally recommends learning experiences that include such management-specific knowledge and skill areas as ethical and legal responsibilities in organizations and society; financial theories, analysis, reporting, and markets; creation of value through integrated production and distribution of goods, services, and information; group and individual dynamics in organizations; statistical data analysis and management science to support decision making throughout an organization; information technologies relevant to organizations and economies; domestic and global economic environments of organizations; general management skills that develop leadership, applications of disciplinary knowledge, and problem-solving abilities; and specialized knowledge of theories, models, and tools relevant to their specialty field (Association to Advance Collegiate Schools of Business, 2004, pp. 15–17).

American and international business schools are the primary mass producers of graduates from traditional M.B.A. programs and from new models that are modular in structure, offered through asynchronous networks or corporate sites and by for-profit companies. More than one thousand corporate colleges for virtually every industry spend "2.5 percent of payroll on learning, double the U.S. national average" and employ the latest in technology to deliver programs that are continuous, immediate, and economical (Crainer and Dearlove, 1999, p. 197). These corporate colleges range from McDonald's Hamburger University, with ten international training centers and programs delivered simultaneously in twenty-two languages, to Disney University, which trains its forty thousand employees in corporate culture, motivation, teamwork, and customer service, to Motorola University, which requires every employee to undergo at least forty hours of training and has its own international M.B.A., to Intel University, which has a $150 million budget and offers twenty-six hundred courses (pp. 196–198).

For-profit companies offer proprietary M.B.A. programs that have become major competitors of more traditional business schools. The University of Phoenix, the Institute for Professional Development, the College of Financial Planning, and Western International University, all of which are owned by the Apollo Group, a publicly traded corporation, boast fifty-one campuses and ninety-one learning centers in thirty-three states, Puerto Rico, and the United Kingdom (Crainer and Dearlove, 1999, p. 216). They use part-time adjunct faculty, virtual classrooms, and Internet advertising to attract thousands of new students to their fast-track M.B.A.s. DeVry, Inc., another publicly traded company founded in 1931 by an inventor and teacher at Bell & Howell, is the holding company for nineteen campuses of the DeVry Institute of Technology and thirty-five sites of the Keller Graduate School of Management, which enrolls six thousand students in M.B.A. programs in business, accounting, human resources, management, and marketing as well as master's programs in information technology and education (Ruch, 2001). According to Ruch, Wall Street analysts consider Dennis Keller, DeVry's chair, and Ron Taylor, its chief operating officer who bought the DeVry operation from Bell & Howell in 1987, to be "one of the strongest management teams in the industry" (p. 44).

Formidable competition from corporations and for-profit companies has motivated universities to extend their strategic partnerships with business and industry, offering modular executive management degrees (the Executive M.B.A.), realigning their mission and reward systems, and recruiting "star" professors who may also sit on corporate boards, advise corporate clients, address corporate groups, and publish trade books that promote managerial strategies and proficiencies. Technological advances facilitate the connections between business and education and the recruitment of new student clienteles. Successful E.M.B.A. programs are more apt to be multidisciplinary, modular, and flexible in the use of delivery systems, staffed by faculty from relevant departments, and tailored "to meet the particular needs of the client company" (Lorange, 2002, p. 71). In a handbook on designing management education programs, Peter Lorange, president of the International Institute of Management Development (IMD) in Lausanne, Switzerland, and a former dean of the Wharton Business School, offers a model for "creating tailor-made programmes" that exemplifies how closely aligned the professional M.B.A. has become with the corporate marketplace, making it difficult to distinguish its stakeholders from the employers they serve (p. 73). Step 1 analyzes the CEO's vision, priorities, and human resource challenges; Step 2 calls for "cobbling together a menu of learning activities" weighing on-site, degree-based, or short-term options; Step 3 focuses on who should attend, the curriculum in which they will participate, and the time frame for their participation; and Step 4 indicates the development of rubrics around learning outcomes to measure individual and organizational learning (pp. 73–78).

Several examples of business school–corporate E.M.B.A. programs provide evidence-based research of the integration of master's education and the marketplace. According to Lorange, "Partnerships with client firms are crucial to the success of any business school, but tailored programmes for individual executives—like IMD's M.B.A. programme and Executive M.B.A. programme, as well as the customized M.B.A. programme at the Lauder Institute of the Wharton School—must also be part of the palette of offerings" (p. 111). At IMD, all academic departments have been eliminated, and the fifty faculty members organize themselves into flexible teaching teams (p. 58). Every faculty member has the title of "professor" to further eliminate hierarchy in the distribution of teaching and research tasks (p. 59). Interactive learning is facilitated through information technology and multimedia presentations, allowing students to "follow their own workplace agendas, learning needs, and specific problems" (p. 66).

Other examples of how the business school M.B.A.—particularly the executive M.B.A.—has moved into the corporate orbit include an international master's program in management presented by a consortium of five international business schools—McGill (Canada), INSEAD (European Union), Indian Institute of Management (India), Hitosubashi University (Japan), and the University of Lancaster (United Kingdom)—and ten companies, including Fujitsu, Lufthansa, Matshushita, Royal Bank of Canada, and Alcan (Crainer and Dearlove, 1999, p. 31). This part-time, fast-track degree enrolls experienced managers sponsored by their companies, offering them five two- to three-week modules structured around "managerial mind-set, collaborative mind-set, and catalytic mind-set" (p. 31). Duke's Fuqua Business School initiated its E.M.B.A. in 1996, sending students for two-week mandatory sessions to Eastern Europe, Asia, and Latin America as well as throughout the United States and Europe (p. 90). At NYU, an E.M.B.A. begun in 1982 provides advanced management study for middle-level managers in production, engineering, or marketing (Gitlow, 1995, p. 151). Structured for students' convenience, the program is two years in length, meets Fridays and Saturdays, and requires employer support, ten years of work experience, a satisfactory GPA, and solid GMAT scores. And at Case Western Reserve, the Weatherhead School of Management has launched an interdisciplinary M.B.A.

specialization in bioscience entrepreneurship as the first stage of its plan to develop a center for bioscience entrepreneurship promoting research and education on the commercialization of bioscience, economic development, and bioscience management (Clark, 2002). Universities located close to major airports such as O'Hare and Dulles may offer courses at airport hotels, flying in students for monthly weekend classes, supplemented by distance learning and Internet communication with program faculty. Dual online degrees linking business with law, journalism, public administration, and engineering may also be promoted in reaching out to new student populations and enhancing overall profitability. The entrepreneurial, flexible, adaptive E.M.B.A. exemplifies the promotion of expert private sector professionalism. The M.B.A. and E.M.B.A. operate in proximity to the marketplace, realigning the borders and territories that have traditionally defined higher education and practical training. Their ambiguity and relativism further problematize the purposes and policies undergirding master's education.

Accounting

In 1989, the American Institute of Certified Public Accountants (AICPA) proposed updating the accounting curriculum, increasing licensing requirements, and revising the CPA examination. It ruled that, by 2000, legislative jurisdictions would require the completion of 150 semester hours of education and a baccalaureate or its equivalent to qualify for the CPA examination (Evangelauf, 1989, p. A31). Approval of the 150-hour requirement by the membership represented the culmination of many years of effort to secure a graduate education requirement for entry into the accounting profession. AICPA was not able, however, to gain the support of either business or accountancy schools or of state legislators for a master's requirement, and it reports on its Web site that "none of the states that have passed the 150-hour law require a master's degree" (American Institute of Certified Public Accountants, 2004). A survey of 350 accounting department chairs at AACSB-accredited business schools in the United States and Canada further reveals that, although 80 percent of these programs are in compliance with the five-year, 150-hour requirement, the technical focus predominates, particularly in undergraduate accounting programs that combine general education with thirty semester hours of accounting (Shafer and Kunkel, 2001). So it is that the five-year, 150-hour requirement is being met through an M.S. in accounting or an M.B.A. degree, or through a required extra year of accounting and business courses (but not a master's degree).

A report on the future of accounting education sponsored by the Institute of Management Accountants, AICPA, the American Accounting Association, and the five major professional service firms expresses the view of "accounting leaders and practicing accountants . . . that accounting education, as currently structured, is outdated and broken and needs to be modified significantly" (Albrecht and Sack, 2000, p. 1). It expresses concern for the declining quality of students and uncompetitive salaries for graduates, and notes a lack of innovative and contemporary content in programs that should be enhanced to address changes in technology, globalization, and corporate practices (p. 2). Albrecht and Sack recommend alternative structures for academic programs: undergraduate accounting programs designed to prepare students for the M.B.A. degree, combined B.S.–M.S. programs in accounting and finance, and an integrated five-year master's in accounting comparable to the M.B.A. It appears that specialized tracks offered by accountancy and business school programs have become more rather than less technically focused, contradicting the vision of accounting education presented by the AICPA when it authorized the five-year requirement.

Another question that goes beyond licensure requirements for business school and accountancy graduates revolves around the stakeholders themselves—faculty, students, and corporate employers. Does the permeability of borders between business schools and corporations benefit the faculty who undertake consultancies, the students seeking to advance in the workplace, the professional associations and agencies that set the standards, and the corporations that want a well-trained workforce? In their annual rankings of business schools, *Business Week* and the *Wall Street Journal* refer to the increased entrepreneurial focus of M.B.A. programs, the competition from European and Asian business schools, and the high cost of the degree—upwards of $100,000 in the top business schools (Merritt, 2004; Alsop, 2004). They call attention to the increase in business specialties, the incorporation of leadership, governance, and ethics into the curriculum, and the positive impact of field learning rather than reliance on case studies (Merritt, 2004).[7] One challenge that business schools share with other professional schools arises from the disparate research traditions of their faculty, extending from marketing and organizational behavior to economics, engineering, and finance. According to a dean of the Yale School of Management, executives returning for more education want to learn how to improve their job performance and integrate disciplinary perspectives, "hearing about how somebody in finance, say, integrates marketing and operational issues" (Holstein, 2004, p. 10). Accrediting agencies and corporate recruiters express the need for a better balance between academic and practitioner standards and strategic partnerships with the business community, greater use of learning technologies and team projects in real-life environments, increased hiring and promotion of women and minority faculty, realignment of departments to deemphasize specialization and enhance multidisciplinary curriculum approaches, and strengthened outcome evaluations of managerial proficiencies.

Education

Schools, colleges, and departments of education (SCDEs) award the largest number of master's degrees and have been established for a much longer period of time than their closest competitor, the business school, yet education degrees have never achieved the status or prestige of the M.B.A. or such first-professional degrees as law, medicine, or dentistry. Initially, an M.A. or M.S. in teaching was the preferred credential for those seeking positions as secondary school teachers or school district administrators. With the expansion of the community college sector in the 1960s and 1970s, it became the degree of choice for those who aspired to teach in two-year colleges or lower-division undergraduate programs, creating a tiered system of qualifications for college and university faculty. It also served as the midpoint for the Ed.D. or the Ph.D. for those seeking academic careers in schools of education. Harvard, which established the first seminary for teachers in 1831, began offering master's degrees in 1870 and the first Ed.D. or applied doctorate in 1922, partly as a means of bypassing more stringent Ph.D. foreign language requirements.

By 1963, one-fifth of the nation's schools of education offered the master's degree. As teachers colleges were expanded mainly into state universities throughout the decade, the number and variety of practitioner-oriented master's degrees grew proportionately. As a result, the mission of master's-granting institutions came to be dominated by professional rather than liberal arts degrees, while liberal arts and science programs, particularly at the graduate level, were reduced to a subordinate service function.

The nation's thirteen hundred SCDEs have several distinguishing characteristics. Yet as a multidisciplinary professional field, education is not well understood. The NCES classification system for education degrees fails to adequately identify proliferating specializations or to disaggregate the growing number of online education-related degrees. Federal data on enrollments and degrees are disaggregated into thirty-five subfields—nineteen teaching fields that range from bilingual to special education and sixteen other education fields that encompass curriculum and instruction, educational administration, and adult, higher, and postsecondary education (Glazer-Raymo, 2001). Many education specializations have their own professional associations, accreditation agencies, and licensing regulations, dividing educators and practitioners into specialized, often competing professional groups in, for example, educational administration, allied health professions, psychology, and the teaching of special subjects. And unlike liberal arts or business, master's programs in education are tightly regulated by state bureaucracies and depend on the good will of local school districts for placing teaching and administrative interns and graduates, maintaining ties with alumni, and tapping into the market for new students.

Of the 3.4 million public and private school teachers in the United States, 88.5 percent teach in public schools (Snyder, Tan, and Hoffman, 2004, p. 15). In 2000, more than half of all public school teachers earned only a bachelor's degree (52 percent), while 41.9 percent earned a master's degree, 4.8 percent a sixth-year postmaster's certificate (education specialist or professional diploma), and 0.7 percent a doctorate (p. 89). There are also 110,021 principals in American public and private schools, more than half of whom hold the master's degree (53 percent), while 28 percent hold the postmaster's certificate and 10 percent hold the doctorate. Indicative of state certification requirements for employment in public schools, only 1.8 percent of public school principals hold the bachelor's degree as their highest credential compared to 23.6 percent of private school principals (p. 102). State breakdowns of master's degree recipients show the highest proportion of teachers with master's degrees in Connecticut (65 percent), Indiana (63 percent), and New York (68.4 percent).

The elevation of teaching from occupational to professional status has long been a contentious issue, not only because of the regulatory fever that has gripped this field since the publication of *A Nation at Risk* (Commission on Excellence in Education, 1983) but also because, as sociologists of the professions have observed, teaching is a unionized profession with a high level of intervention from the communities it serves through its elected or appointed school boards, parent and taxpayer groups, state boards of education, and the federal Department of Education. Throughout the 1980s and 1990s, state-level and national task forces and commissions conferred frequently on how to "reform" teacher education. The Holmes Group, an association of education deans from research universities, proposed in its first report, *Tomorrow's Teachers* (1986), that undergraduate education programs be eliminated, that all teacher education candidates be proficient in the liberal arts and science, and that state certification be conferred in three stages following completion of accredited master's degrees and a one-year paid teaching induction program. Its second report, *Tomorrow's Schools of Education* (1995), proposed that all schools of education establish professional development schools within local school systems to engage preservice teachers in actual classroom experiences and to bring classroom teachers to college campuses as adjunct faculty in schools or departments of education. The main goal of this model was the professionalization of preservice and in-service teachers, a concept that its proponents soon found would require expert direction, continuous oversight, and substantial resources to implement successfully. Another task force report, *A Nation Prepared* (Carnegie Task Force on Teaching as a Profession, 1986), added its imprimatur to admonitions that the undergraduate degree in education be eliminated as a means of raising the status and quality of teachers. It proposed conferral of a new master's degree—the Master of Science in Teaching (M.S.T.)—as a requirement for initial teacher certification. This degree is a variation of the Master of Arts in Teaching (M.A.T.), which had combined a modicum of education courses with year-long internships in local schools for the purpose of encouraging talented graduates of select liberal arts colleges to become public school teachers. Although still offered to secondary teaching candidates in selective institutions such as Brown University and Stony Brook University, the M.A.T. has had only minimal impact, a small ripple in the larger ocean of education degrees. A similar fate has befallen the M.S.T. as a result of a lack of name recognition and the perception among teachers and teacher educators that education degrees should adhere to the more commonly understood designations, particularly in a profession with more than fifty specialties (as noted in the NCES taxonomy).

A more pervasive goal has been to professionalize teaching by promoting a national licensing examination for master teachers, promulgating model standards that promote teacher quality, and encouraging schools of education to obtain national accreditation of their programs. Several major actors in the educational establishment have been working together to promote the professionalization of teachers, setting up the apparatus to obtain the necessary resources, gain political support, and foster organizational change. The National Board for Professional Teaching Standards (NBPTS) and the Interstate New Teacher Assessment and Support Consortium (INTASC) were both initiated in 1987 for this purpose. Through the National Governors Association, the Education Commission for the States, and other organizations, policies have been formulated and projects advanced. The master's degree is a pivotal step toward professionalization of teaching.

The NBPTS operates in tandem with individual states to recognize teacher professional development, and the advanced master's degree is one of its stated goals (Isenberg, 2003). A substantial sum, $300 million, has been awarded to the NBPTS since its establishment, and a number of incentive and recognition programs for NBPTS-certified teachers are in place in all fifty states and in five hundred school districts (Goldhaber, Perry, and Anthony, 2004). Since 1994–1995, NBPTS has administered voluntary examinations in thirty educational specialties for advanced certificates valid for a period of ten years and renewable through additional testing. The test is costly, however, requiring three hundred hours of preparation and a $2,300 application fee, and by 2004, only thirty-two thousand of the 3.3 million public and private school teachers in the United States had taken it. Impetus for greater participation, however, may come from the bonuses and merit pay increases offered to nationally certified teachers as well as the perception that "by defining professional standards and recognizing 'master' teachers," NBPTS is encouraging SCDEs to strengthen their teacher preparation programs (p. 261).

A recent NBPTS report (Isenberg, 2003) offers criteria for developing high-quality master's programs, descriptions of several model programs, and optimistic predictions for reshaping the master's from a basic to an advanced credential. Many state boards of education also address the basic versus advanced model of teacher education by requiring the master's degree or fifth-year of study in teacher education combined with the fulfillment of content requirements in the liberal arts. A recurrent issue is the reluctance of faculty in many colleges of arts and science to address the needs of either public schools or two-year colleges, the primary employers of master's-level graduates. In some states, Colorado among them, education departments are responding with mandates that secondary education specialties be housed in colleges of arts and science rather than in schools of education. In other states, education faculty tend to keep arts and science faculty at arm's length, relying instead on their own content area specialists to teach and supervise master's students. This duplication of effort highlights the difficulties of restructuring for quality assurance purposes and the role of the state in making determinations about the content of professional programs.

INTASC was created by a consortium of state education agencies and national education organizations. It promulgates ten model standards that conceptualize the teaching and learning knowledge base for beginning teachers and promote teacher professional development based on research that "the strongest predictor of students' achievement is the percentage of well-qualified teachers in a school, district or state" (Darling-Hammond, 1998, p. 8). Proponents of standards highlight the disproportionate number of newly hired unlicensed teachers in urban and low-income schools and in fields such as mathematics, life science, and physical science (pp. 8–9). Model programs incorporating INTASC standards stress fieldwork, theory-into-practice teaching and learning, reflective practice, and continuous clinical experiences.

Proponents of the INTASC standards include the National Council for Accreditation of Teacher Education (NCATE). Established in 1954, this major accrediting body for teacher education gains support from a powerful coalition of thirty-three specialty professional associations, teacher educators, content specialists, and local and state policymakers, including the American Federation of Teachers (AFT), American Association of Colleges of Teacher Education (AACTE), National Association of State Boards of Education (NASBE), National Education Association (NEA), and national councils of social studies, English, science, and teachers of English to speakers of other languages (TESOL). Approximately 545 colleges and departments of education have gone through the NCATE accreditation process, which is now being piloted on the Web in twenty-five institutions.

In 2003, a second accrediting body was approved by the federal Department of Education—the Teacher Education Accreditation Council (TEAC). Initiated as a direct alternative to NCATE by the Council of Independent Colleges, it is supported by the Association of American Universities, the National Association of Independent Colleges and Universities (NAICU), the National Association of State Universities and Land-Grant Colleges (NASULGC), and the American Association of State Colleges and Universities (AASCU). Education now has the distinction of not one but two official accreditation bodies having widely divergent standards. TEAC is more flexible than NCATE in allowing schools of education to set their own professional standards and requiring them to submit an inquiry brief and related documentation as the basis for accreditation. In its short history, it has given seventy programs candidate status and accredited seven. When reviewed in conjunction with state certification criteria, external reviews of teacher education programs have an enormous impact on resource allocation, curriculum design, student assessment, use of facilities, and faculty governance.[8] The reauthorization of the Higher Education Act in 2005 incorporates the Ready to Teach Act, extending provisions of the No Child Left Behind Act and proposing greater accountability in teacher training programs. Much to the trepidation of education deans and faculty, its passage would expand state and federal intervention into the work of SCDEs and the role of accreditors. It would also provide a stronger rationale for the application of national standards, possibly using the INTASC model, and increase the viability of advanced master's degrees for initial certification. Thus, education and business provide striking examples of a dichotomy in perspectives on the role and status of professional master's degrees. As a highly regulated profession, teacher education in particular is accountable to multiple stakeholders for support of its programs and the quality of its graduates. Business and accounting are less apt to be held accountable (except indirectly) for the quality of their programs and the roles played by their graduates in the corporate marketplace. This disparate viewpoint on master's education illustrates the complexities of professionalization in a credential-conscious society.

Professionalizing Science
and Engineering

FUNDAMENTAL BREAKTHROUGHS IN THE SCIENCES and the central role of industrial research in biotechnology and related fields are generating university-business dialogues regarding the appropriate training for the next generation of scientists. Incentives provided by corporations, foundations, and state and federal agencies contribute to this discourse involving faculty and deans in schools of business, engineering, science, and public policy. The Committee on Science, Engineering, and Public Policy (COSEPUP), a joint committee of the National Academy of Sciences, National Academy of Engineering, and Institute of Medicine, elevated this debate to the national level with its influential report, *Reshaping the Graduate Education of Scientists and Engineers* (1995), in which it proposed a broader range of academic options that allow students to gain a wider variety of skills and exposure to authentic job situations, more accurate information on alternative career pathways (including stopping "with a master's degree, in light of their aspirations and projected employment demands"), and a national policy "to deliberately examine the goals, policies, conditions, and unresolved issues of graduate-level human resources" (pp. 4, 5).

In raising questions about the changing context of graduate education, COSEPUP documented two trends: shifts in employment from teaching and basic research to applied research or even nonresearch employment and the acquisition of skills in "multiple disciplines, minor degrees, personal communication skills, and entrepreneurial initiative" (p. 36). Although the report devoted only a half page to "the master's experience," it took note of the fact that in engineering, public health, computer science, and bioengineering and

---

for those who plan to teach in high schools and community colleges, the science master's is a customary and appropriate terminal credential (p. 49). As a result of COSEPUP's report on graduate education in the sciences, new programs emerged to prepare the future workforce. Most of them focused on the doctorate and the preparation of future faculty, including the Carnegie Initiative on the Doctorate, the Woodrow Wilson Project on the Responsive Ph.D., the Re-Visioning the Ph.D. Project, the Burroughs Wellcome Interfaces Program, the CGS/AACU (Association of American Colleges and Universities) Preparing Future Faculty Program, the National Science Foundation's (NSF's) Alliance for Graduate Education and the Professoriate, and the Integrated Graduate Research and Education Traineeship Program. These and other graduate reform projects were summarized at an NSF workshop on innovations in graduate education (Lorden and Slimowitz, 2003). Only two of the projects mentioned in this summary address master's education: the Sloan Professional Master's Program and the NSF Graduate Fellows in K–12 (GK–12).

An analysis of the literature in science and higher education highlights a trend away from disciplinary hypothesis-based research to problem-based, interdisciplinary studies that address commercial and societal needs, generate context-specific knowledge, and bring together life scientists, physical scientists, and social scientists, frequently in consortial arrangements or partnerships that operate in academic or nonacademic settings (Gibbons and others, 1994; Kumar, 2003; Palmer, 2001). In her investigation of how scientists work across disciplines to solve research problems, Palmer (2001) provides a rich narrative account of the strategies used by scientists in an interdisciplinary research center made up of 150 faculty as well as visitors from other universities, government, and industry, postdoctoral fellows, and graduate and undergraduate students (p. 3). Although this study does not focus on master's education, Palmer's informants observed that to work across disciplines would require "a tremendous amount of training" to bridge the abstract mathematical and physical worlds of traditional scientific fields and to fully use sophisticated computational technology (p. 49). She quotes a scientist who had worked in the aerospace industry that he would not recommend an interdisciplinary research track for students planning to work within university structures but that interdisciplinary training would be more appropriate for graduate students planning to enter industry "where researchers with an interdisciplinary orientation [are] valued and rewarded" (p. 50). These observations regarding the preparation of graduate students for the scientific workforce suggest the need for what is sometimes referred to as "STS approaches" that integrate science, technology, and society, fostering pedagogical content knowledge and value-laden learning contexts (Baerwald, 2003). This thought is reflected in NSF's long-term strategic plan "to identify and provide long-term support for new and emerging opportunities within and across all fields of science and engineering, including interactions between and among disciplines . . . [and] to encourage cooperative research and education among disciplines and organizations, across different sectors, or across international boundaries" (p. 15). A report on trends in federal support of research and graduate education also calls attention to the interdisciplinarity of scientific research, citing "genomics and bioinformatics [that] rely on mathematics and computer science as much as biology for progress; nanotechnology, which depends on chemistry and chemical engineering, physics, material science, technology, and electrical engineering; and understanding of climate change, which relies on collaboration among oceanographers, atmospheric chemists, geologists, geophysicists, paleontologists, and computer scientists" (Merrill, 2001, p. 87).

The Biosciences

Both bioinformatics and biotechnology demonstrate how industrial connections between basic and applied science are transforming the biological sciences and consequently changing the nature of graduate education in the sciences. Building on COSEPUP's recommendations, twelve articles published between 2001 and 2003 in *Journal of Biochemistry and Molecular Biology Education* provide a road map for reshaping scientific and engineering graduate education and training in biotechnology and its related industries. In the inaugural issue, Stephen Dahms observes that academicians "refrain from the terms training, workforce, human resources, skill sets, etc., largely based on history, and often from a lack of appreciation of the industry and knowledge of what their students who elect careers in the industry actually do" (Dahms, 2001a, p. 121). He states further that with the creation of government initiatives to produce "an adequate life science industry workforce" and maintain global competitiveness, research universities in the United States are now exploring the potential of professional master's degree programs and professional doctorates, "starting with molecular life science baccalaureates as the input" (p. 121). Among the topics he discusses are the interface of biotechnology with the pharmaceutical and medical device industries and the role of the M.S. in the bio/pharmaceutical industry. He defines biotechnology as a complex array of scientific and engineering disciplines in which the "techniques of chemistry, biology, and physics combine to form a life science–focused array of technologies including monoclonal antibody, cell culture, biosensor, antisepses, protein engineering, nana, information, quantum computing, proteomic, micro array and recombinant technologies" (Dahms, 2001b, p. 206). Notably, he continues, "biotechnology exists in close union with academia, which not only supplies important fundamental discovery research in the underlying sciences and engineering, but also provides a skilled workforce" (p. 206). One issue concerns companies that seek individuals with "fundamental leading-edge knowledge in the traditional areas such as biochemistry, molecular biology, pharmacology, computational science, and chemistry, but [who] also have skills sets from the dynamic zoo of new technologies" (p. 207). He points out that a number of factors have inhibited the expansion of graduate-level specialized training programs in the new technologies, including the high cost of mounting specialized training programs in science and technology, a general reluctance to extend the time-to-degree at the graduate level, a lack of exposure of future scientists and engineers to alternate careers, and the difficulties of introducing such innovations as team-based approaches that deal with "new concepts of translational research and application-oriented pure research" in industrial settings (Dahms, 2003, p. 201). The biotechnical workforce is currently estimated at 19 percent Ph.D., 17 percent M.S., 50 percent B.S., and 14 percent vocational-community college–trained (p. 199). Focusing on the state of California, where half of all biotech companies are located, Dahms recommends that industry and government work with biotech programs in the California system to develop at least twelve new professional graduate degrees in areas that train the current and future workforce and that these new degrees be "shorter, faster, more focused, industry-responsive educational opportunities . . . deploying company scientists in unique academic–industry partnerships" (p. 201). He specifies that curricula should match company needs, provide internships as part of graduation requirements, and build financial and intellectual partnerships, faculty internship programs, and adjunct practitioner appointments.

A dissertation study conducted at Texas A&M University by a biotechnology program coordinator illustrates the complexity of collaborative planning in the design of a combined professional science master's program in biotechnology and business (Kantz, 2004). Using the Delphi process to identify stakeholders' preferences for various dimensions of a proposed Professional Science Master's (P.S.M.) degree, Kantz conducted five rounds of data collection from twenty-four panelists, equally divided by academic and industrial affiliation. Ultimately, participants selected four tracks for the ideal P.S.M. in biotechnology: preclinical and clinical research, business development, science (cellular biology, molecular biology, and biochemistry), and manufacturing, recommending that programs emphasize hands-on experience, curricula, and assessments that encourage critical thinking, problem solving, communication skills, and both scientific and nonscientific topics. Participants generally agreed on the selection of an industry advisory board to take part in needs assessments, curriculum reviews, internship development, and student job placement (p. 37). Given the emphasis on outcomes assessment in today's climate, this mode of empirical investigation may provide a model for curriculum development, keeping in mind the rapid changes occurring in platform technologies and the vicissitudes of the regional marketplace.

In this new era of the biosciences, such fields as automation engineering and robotics, systems biology, computer science, and informatics are changing the ways in which students are being trained for careers in the applied life sciences. New models of professionalized master's education that diverge from the predoctoral research model are being designed to prepare candidates for alternative paths to scientific careers. This terminal master's in a scientific field is typically a two-year postbaccalaureate course of study, combining coursework with field experiences that correspond more directly with business-industrial needs. A high-demand hybrid discipline that exemplifies the professionalization of the biosciences is biotechnology and its subdiscipline, bioinformatics. A third category achieving prominence is nanotechnology, which NSF predicts will contribute $1 trillion to the economy by 2015 (Feder, 2004, p. 12). Professional master's degrees in nanotechnology include the M.S. in micro- and nanotechnology enterprise at the University of Cambridge, funded by the Professional Practice Program of the Cambridge–MIT Institute, and the Professional Master of Science in Nanoscale Physics at Rice University. Two nanotechnology centers at Rice support faculty and student research in the emerging field of nanoscale science and nanotechnology: the Center for Nanoscale Science and Technology, which involves faculty from physics, astronomy, chemistry, electrical and computer engineering, civil and environmental engineering, chemical engineering, bioengineering, computational and applied mathematics, mechanical engineering, and materials science departments; and the Center for Biological and Environmental Nanoscience, addressing the scientific, technological, environmental, human resource, commercialization, and societal barriers that "hinder the transition from nanoscience to nanotechnology" (Wiess School of Natural Sciences, 2005).

New hybrid degrees are now being implemented in research and comprehensive universities at both the master's and doctoral levels. They exemplify how changes in the production of knowledge influence the design and support of new specializations in the biosciences. A subfield of biotechnology and molecular biology, bioinformatics has gained rapid acceptance in graduate schools of science. Defined as "a mechanism for the acquisition, processing, structured analysis, and storage of biological data" and for integrating these data with knowledge resources from other domains, it may also be subdivided into software development, computational biology, and even library and information science (Samudhram, 2002; Henry, 2002). Some observers suggest that a Master of Science in Bioinformatics combined with a Master of Business Administration or its equivalent may be essential in a competitive job market, particularly in the aftermath of the outsourcing of bioinformaticist positions to India, Malaysia, and other Asian countries (Samudhram, 2002).

Celia Henry's summary of career opportunities in bioinformatics (2002) highlights the symbiotic relationship of science, technology, and business in which data integration, formatting, conversion, analysis, and automation are fostered for purposes of biological innovation. According to Henry's informants, the ideal bioinformaticist may be strong in mathematics and statistics in some industries, but in other industries biochemists, cellular biologists, and physical and computer scientists are preferable. One biotech firm wants a master's degree in biology with some computer skills; another opts for a computer scientist "who can pick up biology on the job." Henry quotes a director of computational biology at the University of Pennsylvania who states that, in addition to knowing the fundamentals of mathematics, chemistry, and physics and earning a doctorate in one of these fields, candidates must be able to work collaboratively in solving complex problems, leading her to conclude that "these different views of what makes a good bioinformaticist means that recruiters have a tough time finding appropriate candidates" (p. 2).

Evidence of its evolving status as an applied degree and the permeation of institutional and disciplinary boundaries can be seen in reviewing the brief history of the Northwestern University Center for Biotechnology, which was founded in 1990 with a grant from the state of Illinois to offer an M.S. in biotechnology. In 1996, it added a business segment by integrating laboratory work with internships in local biotechnology companies. In 2003, the program became part of Northwestern's Kellogg School of Management, changing its name to the Kellogg Center for Biotechnology and its emphasis from science to management. Further evidence of the impact of bioinformatics on professional programs occurs in nursing schools that have initiated the M.S. in nursing informatics, emphasizing the interaction of cognitive science, computer science, and information science in the delivery of nursing care (Turley, 1996, p. 309). Twenty years ago, the M.S. in nursing focused on the acquisition of advanced knowledge in the humanities, science, and nursing theory as the basis for advanced practice and as a foundation for doctoral studies. Here again, changes are driven by the need to acquire computer and software skills that enhance the input, retrieval, manipulation, and dissemination of health care data, and to professionalize nursing and related health care fields.

Degree Diversity: The Professional Science Master's and the Master of Bioscience Degrees

Professional science master's degrees illustrate the realignment of disciplines, the permeation of boundaries, the growth of cross-disciplinary or hybrid fields, and the impact of powerful experimental technologies. As Klein (1993) proposed, the cracking, blurring, and fragmenting of disciplinary boundaries signal challenges and opportunities for rethinking master's education in the biosciences and forming stronger relationships between liberal education and professional schools. The crossing of disciplinary boundaries can be seen in a number of recent projects being implemented with external funding, not only by NSF but also by philanthropic foundations that support science and engineering research. Two of these projects involve the master's degree—the Sloan Foundation's Professional Science Master's (P.S.M.) Program and the Keck Foundation's Master of Bioscience (M.B.S.). Both projects originated in 1997, one with a grant of $50 million to establish the freestanding Keck Graduate Institute (KGI) of Applied Life Sciences and the other with $7 million to provide planning and implementation grants for single-track and multitrack P.S.M. programs in the sciences and mathematics. Both projects link applied scientific study with business and technology in preparing a skilled workforce for leadership positions in corporations and government. The disciplinary foci of the P.S.M. and the M.B.S. may vary in content and structure, but they exhibit several professional characteristics—industrial advisory boards, skills development (communications, technology, and teamwork), business modules, and capstone field experiences. These models challenge the values and norms of graduate education in the sciences, which has traditionally focused on the doctorate rather than the master's, largely overlooked in status-conscious academic science by research faculty directing grant-supported laboratories.

The Master of Bioscience

KGI was founded as part of a seven-college consortium, the Claremont Colleges of California. Its target is to prepare "professionals" for the life science industry through a brand-new degree, the M.B.S. In a short time, its endowment coupled with its single-purpose mission, entirely new faculty, and physical plant has enabled KGI to establish itself as a credible alternative to its public university competitors—the University of California and California State University systems—which must deal with policymakers, governing boards, and academic senates. Its board chair and founding president, Henry Riggs, says that "MBS recipients will be skilled in the practical applications of the life sciences and qualified for a variety of leadership positions in industry" (Riggs, 2002). Its goal is cross-disciplinary, combining scientific training usually gained through traditional Ph.D. coursework with the management and leadership skills provided by an M.B.A. program. Its two-year M.B.S. combines course sequences in the biosciences with bioinformatics, bioethics, bioengineering, pharmaceutical development, and nontechnical courses in finance, marketing, and the business of bioscience. Students also complete team projects and internships in business-industrial locations. A career coordinator locates internships with potential employers in such fields as project management, business development, regulatory affairs, quality assurance, manufacturing, product development, and marketing. In its curricular mission statement, KGI states that the professional M.B.S. "educates a cadre of technically competent professionals for the bioscience industry who can oversee development of useful new technologies, products, processes and services from basic life sciences research, and address the business and ethical challenges of management" (Keck Graduate Institute, 2004). The M.B.S. program was designed initially by a faculty planning group charged with creating a teaching cadre mainly from industry rather than from academia and an infrastructure for active research communities. According to the dean of faculty, its small size and focus on team-based pedagogy have led to the creation of an inquiry-centered active learning experience that distinguishes it from the entrenched research culture of the university (Dewey, 2003). Class projects and interdisciplinary team-taught courses incorporate the latest scientific advances and seek to leverage research and pedagogy to facilitate student learning.

The Professional Science Master's

The Sloan Foundation encourages a broader approach through its P.S.M. degree, a freestanding terminal degree for scientists seeking nonacademic careers. Since 1997, it has provided planning and development funding for nearly one hundred P.S.M. degree tracks in forty-five universities, based on the supposition that gaining acceptance at the top tier of research university science and mathematics departments would enhance the status of the degree. Grants to CGS from the Sloan Foundation also support the planning and operationalization of fifteen multitrack P.S.M. programs at master's-level universities. P.S.M. programs now enroll more than eleven hundred students (46 percent women, 28 percent foreign nationals, and 6 percent historically underrepresented minorities). Among 230 of the 450 graduates, 50 percent work in the private sector (communication with S. Tobias, October 15, 2004). The rationale for the P.S.M. is threefold: to encourage students with science and mathematics backgrounds to gain technological and business skills that will prepare them for nonacademic careers and in the process attract more students to graduate work in science and mathematics; to address the oversupply of Ph.D.s and postdoctorate individuals in the sciences and mathematics; and to train scientists for leadership positions in business settings as laboratory managers and in extra-laboratory roles in sales, finance, and marketing.

P.S.M. programs may be interdisciplinary, multidisciplinary, or single-track specializations in one or more of the life sciences, physical sciences, or mathematics. Of the one hundred P.S.M. programs supported by Sloan, eighteen are single-track computational molecular biology/bioinformatics master's degrees; the rest are multitrack programs in other bioscience specializations, including concentrations in biochemistry, biotechnology, microbiology, molecular biology, pest management, zoo and aquarium management; computational, bioanalytical, molecular, and forensic chemistry; applied and industrial physics; industrial and financial mathematics; geosciences, including geographic information systems (GIS), environmental assessment, and risk management; and medical-related specialties, including nursing informatics, applied genomics, biomedical laboratory operations, and health physics. They incorporate advanced coursework, often in more than one discipline; a basic knowledge of business principles and ethics; familiarity with legal, regulatory, and economic issues; participation in integrative activities that develop oral, written, interpersonal, and technical skills; and internships in business settings. These master's degrees differ from the more conventional M.S. degree, which may be an extension of a B.S. in one of the sciences or mathematics to qualify candidates for a teaching license or a predoctoral degree constituting the first year of coursework toward the Ph.D. in molecular biology, microbiology, genetics, or another specialization.

With support from the Sloan Foundation, North Carolina State University, located near Research Triangle Park, has inaugurated a Master's in Microbial Biotechnology (M.M.B.), a two-year program combining academic and corporate training in business (College of Management), biotechnology and microbiology (College of Agriculture and Life Sciences), and internships in the Research Triangle for a total tuition cost of $8,000. Oregon State University offers degrees in applied biotechnology (leading to an M.S. in genetics), applied systematics (leading to an M.S. in botany and plant pathology), and environmental sciences to train professionals for jobs outside academia (Demyan, 2003). The Center for Bioinformatics at the University of California at Los Angeles enrolls students from thirteen departments of science, engineering, and computer science for a postmaster's certificate in bioinformatics. Michigan State University's seven P.S.M. programs require an intensive graduate certificate in business management and communication skills taught by the School of Management and College of Communication Arts, with input from a business and industry advisory board. Students pay $4,500 for this certificate, which consists of ten two-day weekend modules, including six in business (financial management, legal environment of business, managerial accounting, marketing management, microeconomics, and project management) and four in communications (making work groups effective, negotiation and consensus building, presentation skills, writing, and a special workshop in professional business etiquette). This certificate is emblematic of program packaging undertaken by business schools for corporations, government agencies, and, in the case of Michigan State, for clusters of students in applied science and mathematics. At the University of Arizona, where the P.S.M. is considered an entrepreneurship program, a business sequence funded and coordinated by the business school provides a structured set of courses and practica incorporating business foundations modules in economics, accounting, marketing, management information systems, operations management, and intellectual property; a practicum in project management; and weekly colloquia with scientists from the region.

In 2004, the California State University (CSU) system, with twenty-three campuses throughout the state, commissioned a statewide study of high-tech industrial leaders to determine the extent of their interest in P.S.M. graduates (California Council on Science and Technology, 2005). An earlier study of workforce needs for professional and master's degree recipients conducted in 1999 by the University of California Office of Academic Affairs forecast a generally favorable outlook for individuals with master's degrees in engineering, computer science, education, and business, and generally for programs that include "new types of professionally oriented, interdisciplinary training that build on the University's research base" in science and technology (University of California Office of Planning and Analysis, 1999, p. 43). The University of California report expressed optimism about job trends for architects, urban planners, social workers, and international business entrepreneurs as well as teachers in special education, mathematics, and science (p. 43). The CSU study found interest among companies involved in interdisciplinary or emerging fields having scientific and technological applications. It also welcomed increased university-industry interaction through advisory boards. Questions arose, however, about whether the P.S.M. would siphon students from M.B.A. or science, engineering, and mathematics graduate programs or would be as popular as the M.B.A. or the Master of Engineering degree (California Council on Science and Technology, 2005, pp. 5, 7). The most cogent recommendations expressed the importance of establishing credibility for a new master's in science, producing "employable" graduates in multi- or interdisciplinary fields and developing meaningful exchanges with business and industry.

The first effort to track graduates of P.S.M. programs was conducted by the Conference Board (Simmons, 2002), an international management research organization. Based on a small sample of fifty-nine P.S.M. graduates at nine universities, it found that students assign high importance to internships (49 percent), career counseling (46 percent), employer presentations (43 percent), and group seminars and workshops (43 percent). Most of the graduates were already employed, although two-thirds were still seeking new positions in biotechnology (37 percent) or computer-related industries (18 percent). The majority ranked academic coursework, independent research, and internships as the three most important aspects of their P.S.M. degree. Given the emphasis on corporate culture in this degree and the fact that the majority of graduates seek management, product development, or business ventures (64 percent) compared with research (23 percent), only a third viewed it as competitive with the M.B.A.

Both positive and negative claims are associated with the P.S.M. project. On the positive side, provosts, deans, and department heads perceive the

P.S.M. as a venture capital investment, strengthening their status with state legislatures interested in the economic return on their investment in higher education, the university's ability to attract and retain major corporate partners, and the payoff in regional job growth. For example, the State University of New York at Buffalo has gained visibility and support in an industrial region seeking to reinvent itself as a high-tech center for economic development. In this context, faculty view the P.S.M. as fortuitous in generating financial support to launch a biotechnology degree program. A second claim that makes the P.S.M. attractive is its start-up cost. Estimates range from $75,000 to $300,000, much lower than a new doctoral track, which would be at least $1 million. Multitrack programs are viewed as more cost-effective in personnel (coordinators, placement staff, and recruiters), cognate course development (business, law, intellectual property, communication skills, and computer science), and assessment (program evaluation, tracking graduates, advisory board liaison). On the negative side, faculty have to be persuaded that the P.S.M. is as rigorous as disciplinary M.S. tracks, that it will not devalue the Ph.D., that employers will not view it as a minor degree and therefore of limited value, and that it will not drain scarce resources from basic science and mathematics programs. Other concerns relate to competition with doctoral programs for faculty appointments, student recruitment, assistantships, laboratory use, and ancillary resources.

A more basic question relates to the vagaries of student choice, their undergraduate academic backgrounds, the availability of financial support, and the compatibility of the P.S.M. with their career goals. The popularity of the M.B.A. and the J.D. relate to the perception that these degrees will translate into higher professional status and long-term economic benefits. Although professional master's degrees are increasing in many fields, the number of mathematics and science majors is declining. It may be that a new cohort of science graduates will prefer the corporate workplace to teaching and research. In some cases, students who are already employed in technology or pharmaceutical firms perceive this credential as providing career mobility. Although interdisciplinary science is not a new concept, integrating science, technology, mathematics, and business constitutes a major challenge within traditional departmental structures, emphasizing an industrial rather than an academic focus. From the perspective of science and mathematics faculty and many employers, the research doctorate remains the appropriate standard. Whether or not a genuine synthesis of science and business can be achieved in P.S.M. degrees depends on the confluence of a number of incentives—resources, leadership, marketing, and career opportunities.

Both the M.B.S. at Keck and the P.S.M. are based on the premise that powerful new experimental and analytical tools enhance the potential for inter- and cross-disciplinary research and development and that, in today's marketplace, the two-year master's degree is eminently suited to provide diverse integrative experiences sought by corporate recruiters. According to the coordinators of the Sloan project, "The goal is to produce ten thousand outsource-proof P.S.M. graduates per year." This goal is rather ambitious, given the fact that no plans exist to provide support for implementation and evaluation. The trend toward outsourcing or moving jobs overseas to developing countries, where salaries are lower and proximity is not important, is accelerating. The ability of P.S.M. specializations to swim against this outsourcing tide and develop a sufficient number of new fields to enhance job creation is yet to be proven. If employers are to enhance their innovative and entrepreneurial operations, it may very well be that scientists skilled in product development, management, finance, and technology transfer will themselves become more marketable in an unstable economy.

The Geosciences

In 2003, the American Geological Institute assessed geoscience master's degree programs in the United States (Claudy and Keane, 2003). Geoscience is classified within the field of earth, atmospheric, and ocean sciences, enrolling half of all such students (Babco and Bell, 2004). Of the 369 geoscience departments that offer a master's degree, one-third responded to the survey, a representative sample by program size and geographical distribution (Claudy and Keane, 2003, p.1). The responses highlighted the broad acceptance of a terminal M.S. degree for entry-level and middle-management jobs, a high participation rate for women (47 percent), low ethnic minority participation (3.9 percent), and declining foreign student participation (14 percent). More than half of the programs (55 percent) reported no ethnic minority students, a third had no foreign students, and 5 percent no women students. Students came primarily from undergraduate geoscience programs (70 percent) or from other sciences, including biology, ecology, chemistry, mathematics, physics, and engineering. Only a few (4 percent) had nonscience backgrounds in geography, economics, and business.

Geographically dispersed throughout the United States, geoscience programs are overwhelmingly research oriented (74 percent). More than half of the programs (61 percent) offer the B.S., M.S., and Ph.D. in geosciences, more than a third (36 percent) both the B.S. and M.S., and less than 10 percent the M.S. and Ph.D. (9 percent). More than a third of the departments offer a combination of geoscience and multidisciplinary curricula; three departments are part of interdisciplinary environmental studies programs. Slightly more than one-quarter of the programs include such nongeoscience courses as water law and policy, geographic information systems, proposal design, environmental dispute resolution, applied statistics, management, earth and environmental journalism, environmental ethics, and economics. About three-fifths of the programs have relationships with other departments or schools on campus, either through joint course offerings, access to faculty, or joint degrees with other departments. For master's graduates, industry is the most common destination (47 percent), but a substantial number (28 percent) plan to pursue a doctorate.

A collection of essays, *Geologic Ethics and Professional Practices 1987–1997* (Abbott, 1998), focuses on the American Institute of Professional Geologists (AIPG) code of ethics, the utility of standards and program registration for professional practice, and issues relating to quality control, continuing education, and professional development. Professionalization of geoscience occurs through state-by-state registration or certification of practicing geologists; twenty-three or more states now have these programs in place, and legislation is proceeding in others (Whitsonant and Philley, 1997, p. 104). Two national examinations that assess minimal competency have been created by the National Association of Boards of Geology in thirteen areas that include geology, mineralogy, petrology, geochemistry, paleontology, geophysics, and geomorphology (p. 106). AIPG conducts voluntary site-based program reviews geared toward undergraduate programs (although applicable at the master's level), overseen by AIPG's Academic Education Committee. Because the emphasis of professional practice is state or regional employment, AIPG reports that a survey of geology departments discerned no support for national accreditation, such as that operated by the American Chemical Society (ACS) (communication with R. G. Corbett, October 8, 2003). Geoscience faculty and employers view the master's as a valid terminal degree for employment in geoscience fields and are amenable to using resources to support master's students through research assistantships. This approach does not appear to be the case in the life sciences or the physical sciences, particularly in research universities where laboratory research is the dominant model for training future scientists.

The Chemical Sciences

The NCES taxonomy subsumes the chemical sciences within the broad field of physical science, accounting for 54 percent of all master's and 60 percent of all physical science doctorates (Babco and Bell, 2004, p. 157). Growing interest in the M.S. in the chemical sciences (as well as the physical sciences generally) relates to the job market and a recognition that higher salaries and employment opportunities may be available to master's recipients outside the academic world where tenure-track positions for doctoral graduates are limited. Interest in professional M.S. degrees may also be linked to the availability of resources for defense, homeland security, emerging technologies, and distance education.

The ACS Committee on Professional Training examines postsecondary chemistry education and approves undergraduate departments of chemistry and the certification of bachelor's degree graduates. In graduate education, it produces the biennial ACS *Directory of Graduate Research* and publishes reports on graduate training in chemistry, primarily Ph.D. programs. In 2003, a survey of chemistry departments conducted by this committee identified three goals of master's programs: careers in industry (89 percent), advanced study (73 percent), and teacher training (31 percent) (American Chemical Society, 2003). The majority of master's students attend full time, completing degree requirements (thirty credit hours) in 1.7 to 2.5 years.

Combined B.S.–M.S. programs (18 percent), industrial partnerships (6 percent), distance education, and intensive summer programs provide variations on the conventional curriculum. The Lehigh University Satellite Network, for example, offers distance education in chemistry and chemical engineering at multiple corporate sites. Industrial partnerships include the master's in coatings technology and polymer chemistry (DePaul University), industrial chemistry (University of Central Florida), and environmental and biotech-pharmaceutical science (University of Colorado–Denver). A professional master's in chemistry at Hamline University resulted from a workforce needs assessment; it integrates curriculum content in chemistry with communication skills, conflict resolution, team projects, business, and management (Wilkinson, 2002).

The National Research Council's Chemical Sciences Roundtable, established in 1997, brings together stakeholders who train and employ graduates of chemical science programs. A workshop on graduate chemistry education focused on interdisciplinarity in existing institutional structures and broader preparation of students to assume new roles in academia, industry, and government. Questions arose about the number of schools of science that are adopting fast-track, practitioner-oriented, extradepartmental centers and online modules in chemical sciences; the impact of these alternative structures on academic standards; and proposals to differentiate between a "professional" master's program and a research doctorate. Whether or not this approach reinforces the degree hierarchy that characterizes science in research universities or, conversely, makes the professional master's degree a more attractive option is a recurrent theme in these discussions. As one participant quipped, the master's degree in chemistry is still referred to as a "good-bye present in all, or almost all, of the institutions that offer Ph.D.s in chemistry" (Ernest L. Eliel, cited in Stacy, 2000, p. 86).

In discussing its viability in the chemical sciences, the roundtable participants noted the inadequacy of stipends and assistantships generally available to master's students, the use of the master's as a screening device for admission to doctoral candidacy, and the surfeit of postdoctorates (Stacy, 2000). A skeptical attitude toward master's education also pervades industrial research laboratories and human resource offices of major corporations that often give short shrift to master's candidates, particularly in a buyer's market, viewing the universities as incubators for the cultivation of research scientists. One DuPont executive at the chemical sciences roundtable observed that the graduate school should serve as a training ground for multidisciplinary research to groom students for the transition into the corporate world, spending time "absorbing new science in other areas," engaging in informal exchanges with other scientists, and becoming more analytical researchers and practitioners (Wasserman, 2000, p. 19).

Despite research chemists' reservations regarding the master's degree, it is gaining legitimacy as the ideal candidate for the P.S.M., for example, in computational chemistry. The magnitude of technological change and the contracting academic labor market, which have made postdoctoral scientific study almost mandatory, appear to affirm contextual analyses conducted in the life sciences and the rationale for the P.S.M. and M.B.S. degrees. ACS is the only professional science organization that accredits baccalaureate programs; in 2003, it proposed the adoption of accreditation standards for the master's degree, based on the perception that changes in scientific research require advanced knowledge and skills and that programs are becoming increasingly multidisciplinary in content and structure. This proposal is still under discussion.

Physics

Of the 768 degree-granting physics departments, seventy-two grant the master's as the highest physics degree, compared with 182 granting the Ph.D. Only seven departments have no undergraduate program in physics (Nicholson and Mulvey, 2002). With support from the Sloan Foundation, the American Institute of Physics (AIP) conducted an extensive survey of physics master's degree programs to determine the extent of their professionalization or employment orientation as a result of changes in the labor market and the demand for graduates with scientific and technological skills (Norton, Hammer, and Czujko, 2001). Most physics programs offer only a general academic curriculum; many offer specializations to complement the general track (p. 2). They define a "professional master's degree program" as one that addresses economic needs and students' goals and provides fundamental knowledge and specialized skills that enable them to enter the workplace when they graduate (p. 2). They characterize salient features of professionalism in master's education as promoting networking and bridge-building with industry; exhibiting a multidisciplinary emphasis; fostering negotiated partnerships with industry for internships and hands-on experience; and demonstrating flexible scheduling and team development structures (p. 6). Through interviews and surveys, they identified twenty-two programs that satisfied each of these criteria, seventeen that incorporated many features associated with professional or employment-oriented programs, and twenty-three "new professional master's degree programs" that have recently been established (p. 11). They conclude that three factors contribute most directly to professionalization: faculty strengths, institutional strengths and weaknesses, and the local or regional industrial outlook (p. 12). Another survey of physics baccalaureates found that five to seven years after receipt of the B.S., 25 percent had earned a master's in physics, another science field, or engineering, while 34 percent had no additional degrees (Ivie and Stowe, 2003). Not surprisingly, an M.S. in physics, chemistry, life science, or engineering contributed to their employment opportunities and salary status. The major concern among physics departments appears to be the decline in enrollments of students at both the master's and doctoral levels, a factor that is underscored by the decline in foreign student science and engineering (S&E) enrollments since 2001. More than half of all physics master's degree recipients enter the workforce, and two-thirds are employed by business and industry. One way to reverse the declines may be to consider the career and employment prospects for physics majors in developing new program emphases. The fact that physics baccalaureates are more apt to change majors at the master's level may also indicate the need to cross disciplinary boundaries in designing multidisciplinary options that link physics, engineering, computer science, and other science disciplines. Recent P.S.M. programs, for example, include applied and industrial physics at the University of Arizona, incorporating a physics core with a business sequence, industry colloquia, industry and research internships, specialty electives, and a thesis or final project.

Engineering

The American Society for Engineering Education (ASEE), established in 1893, formed the Committee on Engineering Degrees in 1910, which recommended that degree titles be restricted to the B.S. and M.S. in designated specialties. An alternative recommendation by the Engineers Council for Professional Development, now the Accreditation Board for Engineering and Technology (ABET), subsequently proposed that master's degree titles indicate their specialties, for example, Master of Mechanical Engineering (M.M.E.). Again, in 1964, the ASEE's Committee on Engineering Degrees sought to restrict the degree titles to M.S. and M.E., with designated specialties in parentheses. These proposals failed to gain adequate support, and in its taxonomy, NCES disaggregated the twenty-six thousand engineering master's degrees conferred in 2001 into forty subfields: electrical (28.5 percent), civil (16.9 percent), mechanical (14.8 percent), industrial (9.2 percent), chemical (6.7 percent), aeronautical/astronautical (3.6 percent), materials/metallurgy (2.6 percent), and "other" (13.8 percent) (Babco and Bell, 2004).

Today, ABET maintains four accreditation commissions that perform accrediting functions in four related fields: applied science, computing, engineering, and technology. It took a leadership role in requiring that by 2001 engineering schools seeking ABET accreditation be required to offer experiential curricula and more hands-on, open-ended, multidisciplinary coursework. It also encourages new educational paradigms by assisting engineering disciplines in redefining the first degree for professional practice. The outcomes-based assessment process approved by ABET encompasses both the baccalaureate and the master's degree; under its provisions the Master of Engineering (M.O.E.) can be fulfilled through one of twenty-seven possible combinations of bachelor's and graduate degrees. Licensure requires that the candidate meet at least one of four conditions:

- A B.S. in civil engineering from an ABET-accredited program and at least an M.O.E. in another relevant area;
- A B.A. or B.S. in another engineering specialty from an ABET-accredited engineering program and an M.S. in civil engineering (not necessarily accredited) or higher civil engineering degree;

- A B.S. in civil engineering from an unaccredited program and an ABET-accredited master's in engineering; or
- A B.S. in civil engineering from an ABET-accredited program with at least thirty semester credits of acceptable graduate-level coursework beyond that required for the baccalaureate.

NSF is taking a leadership role in defining future directions for engineering research and innovation through the restructuring of its Directorate for Engineering. The overarching goals of the draft document *Strategic Directions for Engineering Research, Innovation, and Education* (June 2005) call for an increase of 25 percent in support of industrial-academic collaborations, another 25 percent increase for precollege activities, and an unspecified allocation of resources to aid academic and professional association efforts in revamping the content and practice of undergraduate and advanced engineering education including greater participation of women and minority students. It further delineates five "frontier research areas for future support" that, if enacted, would influence long-range planning in engineering education: bioengineering, nanotechnology, critical infrastructure systems, complex engineered and natural systems that include ecosystems, the worldwide web, metabolic pathways, and the power grid—and such manufacturing innovations as nano and nano-bio manufacturing (Directorate for Engineering, 2005, p. 8). The potential impact on engineering education will be to elevate the status of professional programs in engineering specializations and strengthen support for the master's degree as an entry-level credential in the NSF Directorate's priority areas. It may also extend the role of engineering schools in business-industry-government partnerships, as well as facilitate crossdisciplinary and interschool collaboration.

Concern that civil engineers are not being prepared to compete for leadership positions has led to recommendations for raising the licensure requirements to the master's level. Over one decade, the American Society of Civil Engineers (ASCE) Committee on Academic Prerequisites for Professional Practice (CAP3) formulated and adopted Policy 465, "Academic Prerequisites for Licensure and Professional Practice" (see American Society of Civil Engineers, 2004b). The body of knowledge (or *BOK* as it is referred to by the ASCE in its documents) consists of fifteen learning outcomes, based on the premise that beginning civil engineers require greater technical depth and professional breadth. It may be fulfilled by obtaining a B.S. plus either an M.S. in civil engineering (BS + MS) or thirty "acceptable credits" and professional experience (BS + MS/30 & E) (p. 2). The "E" refers to structured engineering experiences that, when combined with academic requirements, result in attaining the requisite body of knowledge. Eighteen civil engineering departments are collaborating on curriculum design projects to critique the bachelor's plus thirty credit hours relevant to the BOK. In addition to noting that this implementation process will take ten to fifteen years, the CAP3 committee concedes that either traditional campus-based courses or distance learning delivery systems will be acceptable for either the master's or 30-credit requirement. It also predicts that "all of the '30' might be delivered through independently evaluated, high-quality, standards-based educational programs offered by firms, government agencies, professional societies, and for-profit educational organizations" and that "distance learning and independent educational programs are likely to become more prevalent and important in the future for both degree and non-degree granting programs" (p. 2). In its policy statement, the ASCE expresses some apprehension that distance education providers can offer high-quality versions of the proposed body of knowledge model "*outside* of college campuses and as *adjuncts* to employee development" (American Society of Civil Engineers, 2004a, p. 2). The professionalization of civil engineering is implicit in its call for greater attention to the environmental, legal, political, aesthetic, and financial implications of engineering projects, and the need to maintain and improve existing infrastructures and to develop new systems. Support for its position has come from a number of professional associations, including the National Society for Professional Engineers, the National Council of Examiners for Engineering and Surveying, and the National Academy of Engineering. Some speculate that disciplinary engineering societies in mechanical, electrical, and chemical engineering may ultimately follow suit, making recommendations for raising professional standards for their members.

A modular master's degree offered by the University of Western Australia provides an interesting case study of how one institution is positioning itself to meet the demands of a specialized field through developing a multidisciplinary Master of Oil and Gas Engineering involving a network of participating universities and industrial firms, and providing grants, equipment, faculty, and jobs (Ronalds, 1999). This two-year M.S. degree offered outside the university structure through the autonomous Centre for Oil and Gas Engineering responds to an industrial need for engineers skilled in developing and operating an offshore oil or gas field. Compulsory modules are offered in science (chemistry, physics, geology, computing), engineering (civil, mechanical, chemical, electrical, naval architecture), and business (economics, finance, management). Students, who attend full time (15 percent) or part time (85 percent), may already have qualifications in engineering and science, serving as junior or senior engineers or managers, with experience in different facets of the industry. Employers include oil and gas operators, design consultants, manufacturing and construction companies, petroleum service companies, and public sector agencies. This new M.S. exemplifies the multidisciplinary and modular approach to master's education more commonly employed outside the United States. It involves fourteen departments and research centers across seven faculties of three core universities.

S&E Degrees in Context

NSF reports "a new peak of nearly 455,400 students enrolled in graduate S&E programs in 2002, a six percent gain from 2001 and a five percent gain from its previous high in 1993" (Thurgood, 2004, p. 1). In terms of master's students, nearly 27 percent of full-time S&E graduate students were enrolled for the first time, an increase of 5 percent (p. 1). And for the first time in many years, the number of non-U.S. citizens with temporary visas enrolled in S&E programs shows signs of diminution. Concern about the employment market for S&E graduates of doctoral programs at a time when the frontiers of science are expanding has prompted educational philanthropies, scientific employers, and federal agencies to offer incentives to research and master's-granting universities for reconceptualizing their graduate programs. Biotechnology, genomics, proteomics, robotics, and nanoscience promise to keep the spotlight on scientific research and development. It is uncertain that science faculty who have been acculturated to the research paradigm in their respective fields will perceive a professionalized master's curriculum as responsive to their needs, interests, and standards. The master's degree, however, continues to be an acceptable credential in computer science, geoscience, and engineering. Moreover, master's-granting institutions are more amenable than research universities to explore the potential of terminal master's degrees in the sciences and to actively recruit students, providing them with the requisite support systems in S&E programs. To some extent, the changing demographics of student enrollments, the industrial outlook and access to internship and job opportunities, and the availability of federal funding for merit fellowships and other forms of financial aid will also guide them in the decision-making process.

Mixed Trends in the Humanities and Social Sciences

S PORADIC ATTEMPTS TO REFOCUS THE HUMANITIES and the social sciences into more practice-oriented master's degrees in the past three decades have been motivated by the shift in undergraduate enrollments from the traditional liberal arts subjects toward technical and business majors, the overproduction of Ph.D.s, and a concomitant decline in the number of tenure-track faculty positions. In addition to retrenching the number of doctoral candidates admitted into humanities and social science programs each year, faculty are being encouraged to collaborate with colleagues in professional fields in preparing students for nonacademic careers. Among the proposals being made are dual master's degrees that link the M.A. or M.Phil. in a humanistic discipline with a professional degree in business, journalism, library science, law, or even medicine, and the improvement of teacher preparation programs by integrating pedagogical content courses into liberal arts departments and eliminating separate tracks for M.Ed. students who plan to teach in secondary schools. And although the dual degree acquired legitimacy in many universities through informal collaborative projects, faculty in research universities have been less sanguine than their colleagues in master's-granting institutions about blending the humanities or social sciences and business, public policy, or education curricula into more professionalized degrees. In contrast to the natural sciences, humanities faculty in particular view professionalization as contested terrain, a manifestation of the debate between cultural critics and literary traditionalists (Graff, 1992; Himmelfarb, 1994; Kernan, 1997). Thus, they have moved cautiously in developing terminal master's programs for graduate students seeking nonacademic careers.

Concern about enrollment declines in the humanities and social sciences in the current decade is prompting more extended dialogues about the professionalization of graduate education within the Modern Language Association, the American Historical Association, the American Studies Association, and the American Economic Association, to name only a few associations that have organized task forces for this purpose. The intense pressure on graduate students to publish, teach, and diversify their interests in response to their diminished career potential in the academy contributes to the high attrition rates from Ph.D. programs, the sometimes grudging introduction of professional development modules to train teaching and research assistants, and the formation of graduate student unions. The humanities and the social sciences demonstrate that the professionalization of graduate education is gradually transforming the norms and values of liberal arts disciplines in response to societal and workplace demands.

To exemplify these trends, this chapter discusses recent developments in humanistic studies (languages and literature, history, and philosophy), social sciences (economics, geography, and public affairs and administration), and interdisciplinary programs in liberal studies, American studies, and women's studies. Two of them, geography and public affairs and administration, have been particularly influenced by technological advances that are transforming the content and delivery systems for these degrees. Both economics and public administration have strong connections with the M.B.A. and in some universities may be housed in schools of business. Women's studies provide an excellent example of interdisciplinarity in actual practice, grounded in feminist theory building, critical methodologies and pedagogies, and curriculum transformation across the disciplines. Beyond the sciences, changes in the content and context of master's education in the humanities and social sciences is evolving into a more professionalized mission for the master's degree. In the humanities, interdisciplinarity occurs in the joint development of centers for bioethics and society. In the social sciences, which have had a more symbiotic relationship with the professions in political science, economics, anthropology, and sociology, departments are extending their reach into multidisciplinary fields of international affairs, public policy, museum studies, and gerontology. With support from the Ford Foundation, CGS is promoting the development of the Professional Master of Arts (P.M.A.) in the humanities and social sciences. In 2005, CGS made twenty-six two-year implementation grants to establish terminal P.M.A. programs in such areas as human language technology, biopharmaceutical economics, museum studies, genetics and research ethics, geographic information systems, arts and cultural management, applied behavioral analysis, and applied gerontology (communication with L. Sims, May 5, 2005).

Humanistic Studies

This section focuses attention on the two largest and most diverse humanities fields—English and history—which are at the center of the arts and science enterprise. It also reviews changes occurring in philosophy and their applications in professional disciplines.

Language and Literature

In the 1980s, concern about the underemployment of humanists in academe resulted in a plethora of proposals to prepare humanists for nonacademic jobs (see, for example, May and Blaney, 1981; Solmon, Kent, Ochsner, and Hurwicz, 1981). Recommendations included revising the content of doctoral programs to make them more practical by adding business and management courses, introducing an internship into graduate humanities coursework, requiring applicants to have prior work experience, establishing postdoctoral business-related programs, or requiring two master's degrees, one in a humanities field and the other an M.B.A. or other professional credential (Solmon, Kent, Ochsner, and Hurwicz, 1981, p. 59). If anything, the underemployment of Ph.D.s has escalated in the past two decades as a result of higher costs of graduate education, the further decline in tenure-track faculty positions in research and master's-granting universities, and the consequent attrition of graduate (as well as undergraduate) enrollments.

In 2003, the Modern Language Association (MLA) formed an ad hoc committee on the professionalization of Ph.D.s to respond to students' concerns regarding pressures to publish before completion of the doctorate but also to heighten awareness of workplace realities for degree recipients in languages and literature, acknowledging that graduates increasingly enter careers in the "business, government, and not-for-profit . . . sector" (Modern Language Association Ad Hoc Committee, 2003, p. 2). This report followed up on recommendations made in 1997 by the MLA Committee on Professional Employment, whose final report contained a self-study guide for evaluating doctoral programs but also included relevant questions for the master's degree in doctoral-granting institutions (Wright, 2004, p. 31). Stating that "the odds of new PhDs in language and literature finding full-time employment in their fields immediately after graduation is no better than 50–50," it quotes Robert Weisbuch, former president of the Woodrow Wilson Foundation, as urging "fieldwide recognition of employment opportunities for humanities PhDs" in the business, government, and not-for-profit sector (Weisbuch, cited in Modern Language Association Ad Hoc Committee, 2003, p. 4). In equating professionalization with the process of socializing graduate students to the skills, identities, norms, and values associated with specialized literary study, the MLA report fails to address the concerns of graduate students who opt for a terminal master's degree in light of what Weisbuch acknowledges to be "30 years of underemployment in the humanities" (p. 4). As Guillory (2000) observes, the realities of the academic job market translate into departmental or college-wide teaching positions that are "largely composition and largely remedial" rather than to "the possibility of a life of continuous research" (p. 1159).

Nevertheless, it is primarily the master's-granting institutions that have been in the vanguard of efforts to strengthen and professionalize the M.A. in humanistic studies, incorporating into academic departments and divisions journalism and mass communications, film studies, creative and technical writing, English as a second language, and applied linguistics, designing multidisciplinary majors that take advantage of departmental faculty strengths, and exploiting institutional resources as a means of attracting students to their departments. Wright surveyed English departments in thirteen colleges of the nation's three largest multicampus systems: California State University (seven), the State University of New York (three), and the City University of New York (three in 2000). She found that in the CSU system, the majority of students sought the M.A. as a qualification for entry-level teaching positions in California's community colleges (Wright, 2004). In New York State, however,

M.A. programs in English were more likely to attract teacher education candidates seeking the degree to qualify for permanent certification in a teaching field (p. 35). Based on her analysis of the MLA *Self-Study Guide for Doctoral Programs,* Wright recommends that English departments with M.A. programs do more to establish informal and formal relationships with other departments and community organizations as a means of creating and augmenting the career objectives of students and facilitating their placement in academic and nonacademic jobs. Data from the 1999 National Survey of Postsecondary Faculty support the view that community colleges in many of the most populous states (for example, California and Texas) are a fertile source of teaching positions for M.A. recipients. The survey shows that two-thirds of full-time faculty in public community colleges have a master's degree, compared with one-fifth with a doctoral degree, one-eighth a bachelor's degree, and less than one-tenth a professional degree (Rifkin, 2003).

Perhaps the most explicitly professional M.A. or M.S. often housed in language and literature departments is English as a second language or applied linguistics. According to a director of TESOL programs, some schools call their program "applied linguistics," connoting a more linguistic focus and placement in a college of arts and science, either in a linguistics or English department. Other schools refer to the programs as TESOL, housing them in English education or TESOL/bilingual education departments within schools of education. TESOL, Inc., reports on its Web site that more than three hundred universities in the United States and Canada offer the M.Ed. or M.S. in TESOL, the M.A. or M.S. in applied linguistics, the M.A. in English with an emphasis in TESOL, or the M.A.T. in English as a second language. In many master's-granting universities where candidates for state certification as TESOL teachers must earn education degrees or additional certificates in English as a second language, programs may be offered jointly by schools of education and colleges of arts and science through a combination of thirty to thirty-six credit hours of coursework, an optional thesis, and supervised teaching practice.

History
In 1965, John Snell, research director of the Committee on Graduate Education for the American Historical Association (AHA) and graduate dean at

Tulane University, conducted a study of the master's degree that found major inconsistencies in admissions and degree requirements, curriculum, and standards. His recommendations for reforming the graduate training of historians, including history teachers, occurred during the great expansion of American higher education when state colleges were being merged into large multicampus systems and federal aid was becoming available for a number of new categorical programs, including the preparation of teachers in the language arts and social studies. The appropriate training for social studies teachers and the promulgation of national and state standards in history, government, economics, civics, and social studies more generally has continued to be a debatable issue within schools of education, colleges of arts and science, and major professional associations, including the National Council of Teachers of Social Studies, the American Historical Association, and the American Political Science Association.

For the past two decades, a number of studies have concluded that reforms were needed in the curriculum and teaching of history. The Bradley Commission on History in Schools, formed in 1987 by a group of historians and history educators, articulated its recommendations in *Building a History Curriculum: Guidelines for Teaching History in Schools,* followed by the establishment of the National Council for History Education, which has published a revised and updated edition of the report (National Council for History Education, 2000). A number of state and foundation-sponsored initiatives also focused attention on the pedagogical content knowledge of teachers of history and social studies, methods of evaluating and assessing students' achievement, and the role of the cross-disciplinary master's degree in strengthening history education. Most recently, the No Child Left Behind Act of 2001 contained in the reauthorization of the Elementary and Secondary Education Act has been the centerpiece of efforts to "close the achievement gap with accountability, flexibility, and choice, so that no child is left behind" (U.S. Department of Education, 2004). Designed to improve academic achievement of children at all grade levels, it also affects the preparation, recruitment, and training of teachers and principals in all disciplinary fields. It is influencing professors in humanistic and social science disciplines to focus much more directly on the curricular implications of its provisions through texts and related materials that are published and disseminated, the knowledge base of its incoming students, and the outcomes of its undergraduate and graduate programs.

The AHA is taking a proactive stance as stewards of the discipline, bringing together historians and educators to assess the competencies and credentials for excellence in the history profession[9] and publishing an analysis of the current status of the master's degree in history (Katz, 2005). In 2003, with support from the Ford Foundation, it formed the Committee on the Master's Degree to examine the current status of and future prospects for the M.A. in history (Katz, 2003a). It followed the work of the AHA's Committee on Graduate Education, which had looked more generally at the intellectual scope, demography, and employment of the American historical profession. Its report, *The Education of Historians for the Twenty-First Century,* had focused primarily on the doctorate, but its applicability extended to history departments in master's-granting institutions and alternatives to the Ph.D. in history and related subfields (Bender, Katz, Palmer, and the AHA Committee on Graduate Education, 2004). The Committee on the Master's Degree conducted its own survey of history departments in the belief that "there is a common terrain of knowledge, skills, epistemology, professional understandings, and habits of mind that should unite all historians trained at the master's level, regardless of their intended or probable career paths" and that more specialized training beyond the common core may be required for master's students preparing for careers as secondary school teachers, public historians, archivists, doctoral students, and community college instructors (Katz, 2005, p. 41). It defined the master's degree in history as practice oriented with a scholarly emphasis but not necessarily with an engagement in original research. Based on this premise, it proposed either a broad master's program or a track within a multipurpose graduate program as some combination of practice orientation, research orientation, and teaching orientation comprising five clusters of mastery: (1) a base of historical knowledge that combines breadth and depth, familiarity with historiographic traditions, and the ability to synthesize different perspectives; (2) research and presentation skills, evidenced by completion of a research project (not necessarily a traditional thesis), and familiarity with the tools of bibliography, the use of primary sources, a foreign language, academic and nonacademic writing, and new technologies; (3) a solid introduction to historical pedagogy that considers how learners of *all* ages attain an understanding of history and optimum modes of presenting history to different audiences; (4) foundations for a professional identity as a historian, for example, familiarity with the development of the discipline and the multiple contexts of professional practice; and (5) learning to think like a historian by cultivating "historiographic sensibilities," critical approaches to historical knowledge, historical "habits of mind," and critical and constructivist approaches (Katz, 2005, pp. 42, 43).

As in other liberal arts disciplines, the intellectual content, multiple goals, and intended outcomes of master's-level programs in history vary among institutions. History offers an assortment of master's degrees—the M.A. or M.S., the M.A.T. or M.S.T., and the M.Ed. At master's or comprehensive universities, students are more likely to have graduated from the institution's baccalaureate program, to be employed locally, or to be seeking certification as a secondary school teacher in social studies. Given the preponderance of history education programs that prepare history teachers, particularly in master's-granting universities, the AHA report offers its recommendations for teacher preparation programs, including the better use of the M.A. in history (rather than in secondary education) for training high school teachers, discontinuance of tracks that segregate teacher education candidates from liberal arts majors, greater emphasis on content pedagogy as part of every historian's training, and consideration of the AHA's credentialing standards for history teachers. The immediacy of this AHA recommendation can be seen in the fact that in several states and multicampus systems, legislators and trustees have mandated that education degrees be eliminated and replaced by disciplinary programs. Undoubtedly, opportunities exist for partnerships in the social sciences in the preparation of public school and community college teachers.

An AHA task force on public history also conducted a survey of agencies and institutions employing public historians (Katz, 2003b). Public history is emerging as a subfield of history for which the M.A. in history seems particularly well suited. Programs that interact with museum studies, conservation studies, art history, and library and information studies have raised the profile of public history and extended its viability as a professional field. The

National Council on Public History, which operates as a clearinghouse for information on public history, supports a rich theoretical literature and standards of professional practice (Howe, 1993). Nearly fifty institutions offer the M.A. in public history and as a minor in several Ph.D. programs. Interest in historic preservation has been spurred by libraries, museums, historic sites, public and private agencies, archives, and access to advanced technologies. Estimated to exceed three thousand, local and state historical societies and historic properties provide a rich array of resources and job opportunities throughout the United States.

Archival studies provide an example of an evolving professional field that originated in history departments but is now gravitating toward library and information science. The M.A.S. (Master of Archival Studies) is expanding rapidly as a result of the technological transformation of research and public libraries, the digitization of print materials, advances in conservation techniques, and the role of electronic management. The 1994 guidelines for the M.A.S. issued by the Society of American Archivists (SAA) called for core courses in U.S. history (legal, financial, organizational), but the current SAA guidelines distinguish between "core archival knowledge" and "interdisciplinary knowledge," which introduces students to other disciplines and allows them to specialize "in truly cross-disciplinary settings" (Society of American Archivists, 2002, p. 3). Its revised 2002 guidelines call for a strong graduate-level archival education based on core archival knowledge "supplemented by knowledge drawn from other disciplines, such as history, sociology, anthropology, economics, and/or library and information science" (p. 2). In this revamped curriculum, history and historical methods become one of eight components that also include information technology, conservation, management, organizational theory, liberal arts and sciences, and library science (pp. 6, 7). SAA acknowledges the variety of existing programs to prepare generalists in archival administration or specialists in electronic records management, historical manuscripts, and the management of institutional archives. The professionalization of archival studies is evident in the new guidelines, which emphasize skills development and technical rather than liberal arts content knowledge, ethical standards of practice, and organizational management. SAA states that possible career paths include managerial or specialized archival work in libraries, historical societies, government and institution archives, and high-tech enterprises (p. 10). Some major themes synthesized from the AHA survey, the SAA guidelines, and related documents focus on the multiplicity of goals and outlooks for academic and public historians and archivists, the transformative role of technology for the history profession, and the importance of dialogues between academic departments and museums, libraries, historical associations, and government agencies.

Philosophy

A report on the M.A. in philosophy, *The Philosophical Gourmet Report,* ranks the top ten terminal programs for which the master's is the highest degree, stating that "these programs boast strong faculties" in the "core areas and/or moral/political philosophy and/or history of philosophy" (Leiter, 2004, p. 1). Brian Leiter, a professor of law and philosophy at the University of Texas and the survey director, recommends on his Web site that students contemplating a doctorate in philosophy consider enrolling in a terminal M.A. if they have not majored in philosophy as undergraduates or if the department in which they did their undergraduate work is "out of the mainstream" of philosophy programs. In a companion report ranking the top fifty Ph.D. programs in philosophy, he provides information on more than thirty disciplinary subfields ranging from metaphysics and epistemology to political and moral philosophy (Leiter, 2004; Wilson, 2005). It is evident from a review of these reports and a search of "M.A." in philosophy Web sites that master's programs are designed mainly as intermediate degrees to prepare students who want to pursue academic careers in philosophy. Since the 1980s, however, concern about the narrow focus of first-professional programs in medicine, law, and business prompted recommendations that humanistic studies be added to the elective curriculum. Social and applied philosophy have had the greatest impact in this context, leading to the development of interdisciplinary and cross-disciplinary courses and specializations in ethical aspects of the medical, legal, business, public health, and nursing professions. The burgeoning field of biotechnology has fostered a number of bioethics specializations and interdisciplinary master's degrees in scientific fields. Targeted audiences for these master's programs range from third-year medical and law students to midcareer professionals. The Association for Practical and Professional Ethics provides information online for twenty interdisciplinary master's degrees offered through humanities and bioethics centers, as online degrees for midcareer professionals, or jointly with schools of medicine, law, public affairs, business, and arts and science (Association for Practical and Professional Ethics, 2004). Michigan State University offers the M.A. in bioethics, humanities, and society through its Center for Ethics and Humanities in the Life Sciences. Marquette University offers a specialization in social and applied philosophy leading to the M.A. and requiring cognate courses in business, law, psychology, bioethics, conflict resolution, public service, nursing, or political science. Oregon State University offers a Master of Arts in Interdisciplinary Studies (M.A.I.S.) in applied ethics. The University of Pennsylvania Health System offers an M.A. in bioethics through its Center for Bioethics and College of General Studies. McGill University's faculties of medicine, religious studies, and law and Department of Philosophy offer master's degrees in students' base discipline (M.A., M.Sc., or L.L.M.) with a specialization in bioethics. Bentley College maintains a center for business ethics offering an M.B.A. concentration in business ethics. Loyola University of Chicago offers an online M.A. in clinical bioethics and health policy, and the Medical College of Wisconsin offers an online M.A. in bioethics for midcareer professionals. Interest in the philosophy of science is also resulting in collaboration between departments of philosophy and the physical or life sciences in offering master's degrees in the conceptual foundations of a discipline as a preprofessional degree that cultivates and responds to student and faculty interests, for example, the M.A. in the philosophical foundations of physics offered jointly by the philosophy and physics departments at Columbia University.

Social Sciences

Economics, geography, and public administration provide three perspectives on the social sciences. Each exemplifies the interaction of the social sciences, technology, and society in the professionalization of master's education.

Economics
In 1951, Howard Bowen conducted the first comprehensive survey of graduate training in economics. His 223-page report, *Graduate Education in Economics,* reviewed the objectives, standards, curriculum, and outcomes of the master's

degree and the Ph.D. in economics at midcentury (Bowen, 1953). He found a troubling tendency "to belittle the master's degree, to regard it as an unimportant vestige, or even to eliminate it" despite the fact that students were four times as likely to conclude their education with a master's than a doctoral degree (p. 54). In reporting his findings, he admonished his colleagues to reinstate the M.A. in economics as a professional degree signifying "professional competence as an economist" capable of entering the fields of business, government, or teaching in a secondary school or community college (p. 59). In proposing uniform standards for the M.A. in economics, he asserted that admissions requirements should assume basic understanding of the field and that "everyone who receives a master's degree in economics [should] meet the standards [that] that degree should symbolize," including a common core of knowledge, one or two specializations plus knowledge of three additional fields, communications skills, some undergraduate teaching, and a capacity for professional growth and adaptation (pp. 61, 62).

Nearly thirty-five years after Bowen's study, Robert Thornton and Jon Innes undertook a survey of the content and structure of master's programs in economics (1988). They found that in the intervening years, economics graduate programs in American universities had proliferated (almost doubling from 135 to 221) and had changed extensively in content and structure, and, to their dismay, they found that standards had deteriorated precipitously. For example, more than half of responding program directors (53 percent) indicated "no specific prerequisites with respect to undergraduate major or minor fields," a common core of knowledge remained minimal, and the research thesis "to demonstrate professional competence" was rare. They concluded that "the master's degree has been devalued, relative to the bachelor's and doctor's degrees" and that "the erosion of standards" should be "halted and reversed" (p. 178). It is probably no coincidence that the American Economic Association (AEA) established the Commission on Graduate Education in Economics in 1988 to examine the structure and content of graduate education in economics and make recommendations to the economics profession (Hansen, 1990, p. 437). Although the AEA considered studying the M.A. and Ph.D., the graduate committee's eventual focus was on ninety-one doctoral-granting departments (Hansen, 1991, p. 1055). Nevertheless, its findings provide interesting insights on the employability of economics graduates and the diversification of economics subfields in schools of industrial relations, public health and medicine, law, public policy, education, business, and agriculture (p. 1059). A critical comparison of the Bowen and Hansen reports conducted by Coats (1992) identifies some common themes in their mutual concern about the disconnect between undergraduate and graduate programs in economics, the lack of creativity and weak writing and communication skills of students, the need for greater breadth and depth in coursework, and the lack of attention to applied knowledge and skills in addressing real-world problems (p. 343). Coats contrasts Bowen's painstaking attention to the structure and standards of the M.A. in economics with the marginalized status given it by the AEA committee, arguing that "American economics is currently in the grip of a narrowly technocratic species of professionalism that is failing to fulfill the reasonable aspirations of many of its members, including students, faculty (perhaps the middle and older generations), and, above all, nonacademic employers" (p. 348). As an antidote, he recommends internships in business, banking, and government and greater emphasis on the professional competence of economists entering nonacademic employment (p. 349). This recommendation is consistent with Thornton and Innis's findings (1988) that the majority of M.A. recipients sought business or government employment rather than to continue for the Ph.D. (p. 177).

A survey of the master's degree in economics at 334 schools, including sixty-three offering agricultural economics, found that programs offering both the M.A. and M.S. and the Ph.D. in economics enroll more full-time students from a larger geographic area (three hundred miles or farther) compared with master's-only institutions that enroll students who have received their B.A. and B.S. degrees from the same institutions or from nearby private liberal arts colleges (McCoy and Milkman, 1995). As might be expected, these students also receive less financial aid, which may account for the fact that almost a third of master's graduates in doctoral-granting departments continue for the Ph.D. "Thus," McCoy and Milkman conclude, "even though the stated mission and program curricula were not different between Ph.D. and non-Ph.D. departments, the mere existence and interaction with a Ph.D. program housed in the same department appeared to have a significant influence on whether or not terminal master's students decided to pursue a doctorate" (p. 166). In an essay on credential inflation and the incremental growth of the applied social sciences, Collins (2002) asserts that economics has prospered in the competition for student enrollments "by producing analyses for business, investment bankers, and government," particularly in the 1990s when the boom in investing heightened interest in the economic status of sectors of the markets (p. 43). He also notes the rift between the research-oriented and applied sectors. "Among economists, there is a prestigious elite that commands high salaries in the leading economic departments and competes for Nobel Prizes, by formulating esoteric mathematical theories remote from the mass of applied economists tracking the performance of particular firms and industries" (p. 43). His observations support McCoy and Milkman's findings (1995) that graduate students will be influenced by the departmental culture in deciding whether to pursue a master's or a Ph.D. Collins makes a persuasive case that credentialism is a spiraling phenomenon that will continue to escalate in the applied social sciences and, more generally, in American higher education.

Geographic Information Systems

The cross-disciplinary focus of geography programs highlights the connections between social science, natural science, and technology. The term "geographic information system" came into use in the 1960s, following the development of the first industry-scale and computer-based land information system. GIS programs originated in the 1980s as nondegree modules, online learning opportunities, and later as concentrations, minors, diplomas, and certificate programs; by the mid-1990s, GIS master's degrees had begun to be offered (Wikle and Finchum, 2003). GIS now defines a multidisciplinary field of geographic information science (GISci) that bridges such disciplines as "geography, geodesy, computer science, cartography, remote sensing with other information technologies including statistics and computer science" (p. 3). It also encompasses social, ethical, and legal issues in the use of technology. Like the geosciences, GIS programs are more likely than other social science disciplines to admit students directly into master's programs (73 percent do so). They are also more likely to include internships, field experience, multidisciplinary content, and professional or skills training outside the department, for example, in statistics, urban planning, and geosciences. The National Center for Geographic Information and Analysis publishes and disseminates online curriculum and assessment materials, working closely with the University Consortium for Geographic Information Science.

A survey of degree programs conducted in 2000–2001 examined twenty-seven GIS programs in four countries, fourteen of which conferred the M.S. in GISys or the more popular M.S. in GISci (Wikle and Finchum, 2003). The University of Edinburgh offered the first such program through its department of geography, using a modular rather than a course-based approach, in which the first six months of study focus on GIS principles and the next six months on individual research projects leading to an M.S. in GISys. Clark University's M.A. in GISci for development and the environment has concentrations in conservation and planning. A number of interdisciplinary degree models emphasize mapping, geodesy, database management, and GIS data structures. Ohio State's M.S. in digital mapping and GIS is offered through the departments of civil and environmental engineering and geodetic science. The University of Texas–Dallas offers an interdisciplinary M.S. in GIS in digital mapping, geomatics, and surveying that is jointly administered by the schools of social sciences, natural sciences and mathematics, and geosciences and six departments (civil and environmental engineering, agricultural and biological engineering, landscape architecture, urban and regional planning, forestry, and applied science). This contemporary master's degree exemplifies the relevance of technology and its impact in streamlining scientific domains and fostering collaboration and innovation in teaching and learning beyond artificially constructed disciplines.

Public Affairs and Administration

The first Master of Public Administration (M.P.A.) was awarded in the 1950s under the aegis of member institutions of the Council on Graduate Education for Public Administration (CGEPA), a satellite of the American Society for Public Administration (ASPA) (Henry, 1995). By 1960, one hundred graduate programs in public administration existed, mainly small programs housed in political science departments, with enrollments of three thousand students concentrated in about twelve large programs (p. 5). The growth of federal and state categorical aid programs necessitated a trained workforce to administer the myriad domestic social service programs of the New Frontier and the Great Society (1960–1968). As health, education, and social welfare programs grew in size and importance, personnel and human resource directors recognized the need for skilled executives analogous to M.B.A. graduates but with specialized knowledge of government organizations. In 1970, CGEPA reconstituted itself as the National Association of Schools of Public Affairs and Administration (NASPAA). In 1974, NASPAA adopted the nation's first standards for master's degree programs in public affairs and administration, and, after a delay of six years from the date of passage, Congress approved federal funding for public service education under Title IX of the 1968 Higher Education Act. Two years later, NASPAA approved a program of voluntary peer review and publication of a list of programs in conformity with national standards. To enhance the status and prestige of this new field, NASPAA instituted its own professional degree designation, the Master of Public Administration (M.P.A.), and its own professional research journal, *Public Administration Review,* and recruited full-time faculty with expertise in the government, civil service, and nonprofit sector. The traditional M.P.A. is a two-year program of thirty-six to forty-two credits with core courses in applied microeconomics and policy analysis, statistics, and applied quantitative analysis. Courses in public finance, management, nonprofit and public sector management, finance, marketing, and communication may also be combined with a sequence in the economic and political environment of public policymaking and in public sector ethics.

The 1970s became a reference point in the growth and professionalization of public administration, as shown by escalating enrollments—twenty thousand graduate students by 1975—and the multiplication of independent professional schools of public affairs and administration (twenty-nine), combined schools of business and public administration (twenty-four), separately organized departments and degree-granting institutes (thirty-five), and academic departments offering either an M.P.A. or specialization (fifty-two) (Henry, 1995, p. 5). Initial support came from the U.S. Civil Service Commission, the U.S. Association for International Development for research and technical assistance in developing countries, and the Intergovernmental Personnel Act authorizing federal grants and contracts to states and municipalities for professional development, graduate fellowships, and executive loan programs (p. 13).

During the Carter administration (1976–1980), an ASPA–NASPAA coalition obtained support for two programs that directly benefited schools of public affairs and administration: Title IX of the Higher Education Act, which provided several million dollars in federal grants to public affairs schools, and subsidies to government workers seeking M.P.A. degrees under the Presidential Management Internship Program. In 1986, NASPAA's Commission on Peer Review and Accreditation gained official recognition as the national accreditation agency for public administration programs. It established three separate accrediting sections for public policy, nonprofit management, and public affairs and, in 2000, a fourth section for health sector management education. In 1992, paralleling trends in engineering, education, and other professional fields, it modified accrediting standards for M.P.A. programs to emphasize program mission and learning outcomes assessment (National Association of Schools of Public Affairs and Administration, 2004).

The fragmentation and hybridization of professional fields is evident in a permutation of the M.P.A. and the Executive M.P.A. It parallels the Executive M.B.A. in business schools, tapping into the escalating market for professionalizing management in regional and state agencies and organizations. Variations on the E.M.P.A. include full-time one-year programs at the Kennedy and Maxwell Schools; weekend programs complemented by intensive summer sessions (at Carnegie Mellon, Rutgers–Newark, and the University of Utah, for example), and weekend and evening classes only (as at the University of Massachusetts at Boston). It also includes repackaging existing courses as stand-alone executive programs, an effort "to imitate the successful practices of business schools to develop and market a separate program and support system for mid-career students," for example, replacing the internship with work experience and allowing students to use the workplace as an action-research learning space (Cohen, 2000). As in business schools, Executive M.P.A. programs are designed to appeal to the local or regional market, offering courses Saturdays and summers, with course schedules adjusted to meet the needs of executive students and programs that emphasize skill building and policy analysis, public and financial management, problem solving case studies, and, for those with limited experience, on-site internships.

NASPAA lists 250 accredited programs with separate curricula leading to a professional graduate (M.P.A., M.P.P.) or undergraduate degree in public affairs, administration, or policy. These degree programs are all grounded in quantitative coursework (financial management, computer science, and research methods); organizational behavior and theory (leadership, communications, teaming, diversity, ethics, and policy); and professional skill–based training, and internships or practica. The leadership strand in schools of public administration, business, and education may involve master's concentrations that prepare students to assume positions of leadership in schools, colleges, government, corporations, nonprofit agencies, and government organizations. Its stated mission of public service and the professionalization of government administration attracts civil service and professional practitioners, most of whom attend part time, may be partially or entirely subsidized by their employers, and engage in short-term internships and related practica.

Interdisciplinary Fields

Interdisciplinarity is exemplified in the humanities and social sciences with the emergence of area studies, American studies, ethnic studies, urban studies, environmental studies, and women's studies. Area studies gained adherents in the post–World War II era through federal support of academic programs that promoted the study of non-Western cultures as a component of national defense policy. Designed primarily as research vehicles that brought together area specialists in the social sciences and the humanities, they had only a peripheral interest in promoting master's degrees, and when external funding declined, so did the area studies programs. The apparatus was in place, however, through centers and institutes established in the 1960s, and the attention of faculty turned toward other options for crossing the "borders-and-territories maps" that Geertz (1983) and Klein (1993) had so forcefully critiqued.

Liberal Studies
The Master of Arts in Liberal Studies (M.A.L.S.), established initially at Wesleyan University in 1952, constituted an early effort to craft a degree specifically for another cohort of graduate students, those seeking enrichment,

personal growth, and professional development in the liberal arts and as an alternative to specialized, technical, and applied master's degrees. The liberal studies M.A. continues to be promoted as a nonprofessional credential for those who seek advanced cross-disciplinary study and who either do not qualify for a doctoral program or are uncertain whether they want to make that intellectual commitment. In some universities, it has evolved into an eclectic mix of contemporary modes of inquiry; for example, at New York University, students in the John W. Draper Interdisciplinary Master's Program in Humanities and Social Thought select from six areas: art worlds, the city, gender politics, global histories, literary cultures, and science studies. In others, it is an umbrella category for cross-disciplinary and interdepartmental majors that may have originated as degrees for nontraditional students or as area studies programs. For example, in 1995, Columbia University transferred six liberal studies programs from its School of General Studies to its Graduate School of Arts and Sciences, consolidating them into an M.A. in Liberal Studies with a concentration in one of eight areas—American studies, East Asian studies, human rights studies, Islamic studies, Jewish studies, medieval studies, modern European studies, or South Asian studies. The program's Web site emphasizes that these degrees are not meant to provide "specific training for a vocation, advancement in a profession, or preparation for graduate study in a specialty" but constitute advanced study in the liberal arts for those who are not yet ready to commit themselves to "the arduous research and disciplinary focus required for pursuit of the Ph.D. degree."

American Studies

Originating in the 1930s as an undergraduate major to promote and integrate contemporary studies in English and history, American studies draws on multiple theoretical and critical perspectives in the humanities, social sciences, and arts. In the discourse surrounding American studies, the borders between ethnic, multicultural, and American studies have become increasingly blurred. In an ASA newsletter on interdisciplinarity, George Sanchez describes the University of Southern California's program in American studies and ethnicity as engaging twenty-six core faculty and forty-two affiliate faculty from across the university in an interdisciplinary curriculum centering on "questions of race, ethnicity, and difference in American life, with specific concentrations in urban studies, gender and sexuality, cultural studies, and race and religion" (2005, p. 2). An American Studies Association (ASA) task force on graduate education reports that there are now thirty-one M.A. and forty-five Ph.D. programs in American studies, American ethnic studies, or some variation thereof. In its 2002 study, it explores strategies for diversifying the pool of graduate students, proposing "new roles" for the M.A. in American or ethnic studies as a "bridge [program] for students of color" seeking alternative careers as community college faculty (Sanchez, 2003). The report also discusses the development of evaluative criteria and standards of quality for graduate programs in American studies and for the accreditation of American studies programs for high school teaching based on competencies rather than on disciplinary affiliations. The ASA task force has also prompted consideration of M.A. specializations in American studies that incorporate community advocacy and social responsibility to give more legitimacy to the terminal master's in this field (Linkon, 2005, p. 2). Linkon provides an example of a new M.A. at Youngstown State University, reflecting the public policy interests and expertise of its faculty and their belief that "preparing students to create social change requires not only good training in interdisciplinary [critical] policy analysis but also the development of skills and experience in organizing and teaching" (p. 3). She notes that this emphasis on community engagement is compatible with the professional backgrounds of faculty and the interests of students and, more important, can enable them to find jobs "that provide opportunities to live the values we encourage them to embrace" in their academic experience (p. 3). She sees the value of the M.A. as not becoming a "'Ph.D. lite' but rather a training ground for professionals who can put the ideas and ideals of American studies into practice in their communities and beyond" (p. 3).

Lest this action be construed as a function of ideological transformation, multiple other examples occur in humanities and social thought, culture and communications, and, most recently, journalism. Columbia University recently announced the restructuring of its School of Journalism to add a cross-disciplinary and interschool M.A. to its one-year M.S. (Daly, 2005, p. B6). The first new degree in the School of Journalism in seventy years, the M.A.

features four yearlong seminars dealing with the arts and culture, economics and business, politics, and science. Immersion courses in Arabic, Chinese, French, Russian, and Spanish are to be added, according to President Bollinger, whose personal announcement of this new degree signals the importance that Columbia attaches to it.

Women's Studies

One of the most remarkable outcomes of the women's movement has been the development of feminist scholarship in higher education. Since 1969, when the first integrated program of women's studies was offered at San Diego State University (Boxer, 1998), more than 750 programs have been established at both the undergraduate and graduate levels, predominantly in the humanities and social sciences but also in the natural sciences and the professions. In many colleges, women's studies originated as a loose collection of courses taught by departmental faculty, gradually evolving and gaining legitimacy as undergraduate and graduate minors and majors. In her comprehensive and authoritative history of women's studies, Boxer (1998) recounts in depth the origins of women's studies in the 1970s, its transformation and growth through scholarly inquiry "from a movement with relatively limited curricular goals but far-reaching aspirations for reconstructing academic institutions, to a new quasi-discipline challenging existing interpretations, methodologies, and epistemologies" (p. 5). In a brief section on graduate work in women's studies, she notes master's degrees offered by 1972 at Sarah Lawrence College (an M.A. in women's history) and at George Washington University (an M.A. in women's studies), and, in 1982, a Doctor of Arts in Africana women's studies at Clark Atlanta University (p. 43).

Beatrice Thompson (2000) observes in the third edition of *Guide to Graduate Work in the United States* that in 1986, only twenty-three universities offered graduate work in women's studies but that by 1994 there were 111 certificate, master's, and doctoral programs (p. vi). Ample evidence of interdisciplinarity and multidisciplinarity can be seen in reviewing program descriptions and degree requirements. Program emphases range from social and political movements and public policy to women's health and sexuality, visual and narrative culture, literary and film studies, feminist pedagogy and ethnography, and global perspectives on women. Thompson notes sixty-six M.A. and four M.S. degrees offered under a variety of rubrics: women's, gender, cultural, interdisciplinary, Africana, American, and liberal studies. She differentiates between degree programs and minors (twelve), concentrations (twenty), departmental emphases (fourteen), certificates (forty), and at least one joint J.D.–M.A. at the University of Cincinnati (2000, appendices). And at Brandeis University, all graduate degrees in women's studies are structured as joint, highly interdisciplinary programs leading to a Ph.D. in a discipline or as terminal M.A.s. The ten departments involved in this joint enterprise include American civilization, anthropology, comparative history, English, literary studies, music (composition and musicology), Near Eastern and Judaic studies, social welfare policy, psychology, and sociology (p. 6). Professionalization occurs through internships and fieldwork with community organizations, international projects, and coursework focusing on women and development, social welfare policy, the health care system, and teacher education.

The vitality of feminist scholarship is embodied in a diverse number of publications that include eleven women's studies journals, fifteen interdisciplinary feminist journals, twenty-nine international English language feminist journals, and eighty-seven disciplinary feminist journals in twenty-one fields ranging from Africana studies to social welfare (Pryse, 1999, pp. 22–26). The interdisciplinary character of women's studies has evolved as the academic manifestation of the women's movement in the 1970s, stimulated by antibias and affirmative action laws and regulations, feminist critiques of disciplinary scholarship and pedagogies, public support for a women's and human rights agenda, and responsiveness to diversity mandates in interdisciplinary contexts (Boxer, 1998; Glazer-Raymo, 1999; Gumport, 2002). As Boxer (1998) points out, women's studies gained credibility and strength through its receipt of external foundation support from the Ford, Carnegie, Rockefeller, and Russell Sage Foundations (p. 48). It is now an international movement with professional associations serving as networks for course development, professional training, research dissemination, and scholarly publications.

A case study of how feminist scholarship evolved in humanistic disciplines in the 1960s and 1970s, a period of cultural and political ferment, uses knowledge creation to conceptualize the development of a women's studies curriculum (Gumport, 2002). Gumport's data derive from interviews with a core group of thirty-five women faculty who entered graduate school between 1956 and 1980 in ten postsecondary research and comprehensive institutions within one metropolitan area of the United States. In her analysis, she argues persuasively that the history of women's studies (as well as other emerging and interdisciplinary fields) demonstrates the confluence of a number of factors: the scholarly interests of faculty, the intellectual content of the emerging field, and the willingness of the institution to vest new academic departments with degree-granting autonomy (2002, p. 16). In her exploration of the two-directional paths through which women "traversed the disciplinary and university contexts at the same time that their scholarly work in turn shaped the contexts where their contributions came to reside" (p. 27), Gumport attributes the convergence of political, organizational, and intellectual initiatives to the successful implementation of degree-granting programs in women's studies.

The work of Boxer and Gumport illustrates the incremental process through which disciplinary and interdisciplinary knowledge evolves and the intellectual, political, and organizational conditions that influence its trajectory across academic generations. Since its inception, its rigor and relevance have been challenged by critics inside and outside the academy. Feminist scholars have also debated its continued viability at a time when the humanities and the social sciences are feeling the effects of competition with science, technology, and the professions. Two developments indicate that the identity of women's studies is being recast within a larger framework: *Guide to Graduate Work in Women's Studies* (Thompson, 2000) lists the majority of women's studies programs as leading to the M.A. in a discipline or in liberal studies, interdisciplinary studies, or American studies; and the National Research Council identifies feminist, gender, and sexuality studies as an emerging graduate field, subsuming women's studies.

The humanities and the social sciences show quite clearly that a number of trends influence the development of master's education, in particular, the changing perception among faculty and deans regarding the role and status of the M.A. in attracting students to its programs, in the allocation of institutional and external resources, and in promoting cross-disciplinary and interschool collaboration. Changes in the Carnegie classification system from a catchall category of comprehensive institutions into the better-understood typology of master's institutions will elevate the visibility of master's programs and in so doing possibly reduce the emphasis on degree hierarchies. A class of master's degrees in public affairs and administration, geographic information systems, and social work exhibits the multiple characteristics of professionalization in the social sciences and leads directly to positions outside the academy. On the other hand, the majority of master's degrees in liberal studies, American studies, women's studies, and gender studies appear to be dominated by humanistic fields and for the most part display only peripheral references to professions other than teaching.

Redesigning Master's Degrees
for the Marketplace

FOUR MECHANISMS PROVIDE THE IMPETUS for redesigning master's degrees for the marketplace: market mechanisms triggered by a global economy, institutional competition, employer demands, and workplace incentives; the convergence of academic and professional fields of knowledge across disciplinary boundaries; state oversight and assessment typified by accountability mandates, quality controls, and resource delivery; and technological advances that transform graduate study and professional practice. These mechanisms are spurring changes in graduate and professional fields and changing the trajectory of professional master's degrees.

Globalization and the Marketplace

The master's degree has been American universities' most successful export, but the peaceful revolution being wrought as a result of the Bologna Declaration may change the calculus of that equation. In that momentous decision, the European University Association agreed to abandon disparate national degree systems by the end of 2010 and to replace them with a single model combining a three-year baccalaureate and a two-year master's degree.

The Bologna Declaration promotes the realignment and articulation of standards of quality assurance, admissions policies, curricular content, distance education modules, and joint undergraduate and postgraduate (master's) degrees (National Unions of Students in Europe, 2003, p. 44). European Union (EU) countries that formerly served only the intellectual elites of their population have now embraced mass higher education and the global marketplace. Although the Bologna Declaration has met some resistance in EU university systems and American universities have raised objections to completion of a standardized three-year (rather than four-year) baccalaureate for transfers, it is likely that this international arrangement will be in place by 2010, creating a more competitive environment for American graduate schools. Other concerns relate to the uncertainties of economic support from federal and state sources in the United States and the uneasy relationships between higher education institutions and the state in many nations and between the universities and the semiautonomous professional institutes that may prefer to retain their degree credit systems. Political instability, disparate quality, and the uneasy relationships between university systems and the state are among the issues being raised in critical analyses of the risks of globalization in higher education (Neave, 2003; Newman, Couturier, and Scurry, 2004). Throughout Europe and the United States, the fast-track M.B.A., for which admission may be based on work experience rather than undergraduate degrees, is the preferred credential in corporate and for-profit business schools that attract an international clientele. In its ranking of business schools, *Business Week* (Merritt, 2004, p. 83) also comments on the preference among graduates and employers for international M.B.A.s.

Another aspect of globalization that indirectly affects graduate and professional schools relates to changes in the conditions of professional work. In their study of work arrangements of professionals in five fields (biology, pharmacy, law, medicine, and engineering), Leicht and Fennell (2001) use the federal *Occupational Outlook Handbook* (1980–1997) to track four key variables related to employment settings, training and certification requirements, labor market demand, and associated occupational groups. They find that today's workplace is characterized by flatter organizational hierarchies, the growing use of temporary workers, extensive subcontracting and outsourcing, massive downsizing of the permanent workforce, a postunionized bargaining environment, and the advent of virtual organizations and a web of technological interactions (p. 3). Biology, for example, in the past two decades has shifted from the majority of jobs in academia to approximately an equal distribution of one-third each in the drug and biotechnology sector, government agencies such as the National Institutes of Health, and academia (p. 31). Professionals, they assert, may be salaried, unionized, and work in for-profit or nonprofit sectors, government units, nongovernment organizations, research think tanks, foundations, corporations, or universities (p. 11). These changes contradict Bledstein's vision (1976) of a culture of professionalism in which the vertical structure of the university and its degree-granting authority served a symbolic purpose in legitimating occupational status and prestige throughout the larger society. No longer do corporations necessarily reward skilled, trained, and credentialed workers with compensation, pensions, and other incentives. Instead, with accelerated momentum, they relocate their operations to developing countries where labor is cheap and technical training can be provided on site. The value of degrees diminishes in these global contexts. The paradigmatic shifts observed in the mid-1980s (Glazer, 1986) have come full circle, and the academic tribes and their territories described by Becher and Trowler (2001) may be considered obstacles to entrepreneurial progress and profitability. Efforts to break down disciplinary barriers at the master's level are occurring through the infusion of institutional and external resources, the collaboration of faculty, department chairs, and deans across department and school boundaries, and institutional and external support for innovation and change.

Convergence of Academic and Professional Fields

An economist and former dean of the Sloan School of Management at MIT asserts that the twenty-first century will be the century of biology and that research universities will find it in their interest to be active players with multinational corporations in creating and managing a global knowledge-based economy characterized by "leaps forward and interactions between six key technologies (microelectronics, computers, telecommunications, manmade materials, robotics, and biotechnology)" (Thurow, 2003, p. 30). New educational structures that are more responsive to these technologies are emerging in the form of asynchronous networks, for-profit educational companies, and quasi-professional schools that integrate the liberal arts and science as modular courses in creating market-driven master's degrees. Research universities have typically eschewed master's degree designations in the sciences and, at the point of intake, have sought promising candidates for the Ph.D.

Conversely, master's universities have traditionally mounted programs in science that serve as preprofessional credentials for advanced training in the health professions or for licensing as secondary or community college teachers. Powerful catalysts for the advent of freestanding science master's programs in research universities are both technological and political, driven by an overabundance of Ph.D.s and postdoctorates, private foundation support, and the availability of high-throughput technologies. Research universities and multicampus systems are active domains for cross- and interdisciplinary activity, most prominently in the natural sciences but also in the social sciences, humanities, and professional fields.

Accountability Mandates and Quality Control

Quality control is a likely outcome of degree program proliferation now offered largely without regulation through traditional and nontraditional modes of delivery. The professionals, the professoriat, and the state have been among the main constituencies monitoring graduate education. They have also been responsible for its extraordinary growth and diversity. In the 1980s, sixteen specialized accrediting agencies and six regional accreditors existed. In contrast, the Council for Higher Education Accreditation (CHEA) now recognizes eight regional accreditors overseeing a total of 2,953 regionally accredited institutions and fifty-eight specialized accreditors overseeing a total of 18,713 specialized accredited programs and single-purpose institutions (Council for Higher Education Accreditation, 2003). The Association for Specialized & Professional Accreditation (2005) provides a clearinghouse for forty-nine accreditors of specialized programs and institutions. This exponential growth, especially in the for-profit and specialized sector, heightens their influence in program development. Accreditation also provides access to federal funds, particularly for financial aid to students such as grants, loans, and other support, thus facilitating student transfer and articulation with graduate schools and employers. Accountability mandates for public colleges and universities and, in states such as New York, for private as well as public institutions increase pressures for compliance with standardization and conformity.

Arts and science assessment has tended to highlight undergraduate education; in the professions, attention has focused on both the baccalaureate and the terminal master's degree. A recent contribution to the sparse literature on assessment and evaluation of master's education is provided by Conrad and Haworth (1997), who assert that such traditional measures as faculty research productivity, student test scores, and acquisition of competencies are no longer appropriate measures for determining program quality. In its place, they identify five clusters of seventeen attributes of quality for use in evaluating undergraduate and master's programs: diverse and engaged participants; a participatory culture; interactive teaching and learning; connected program requirements; and adequate resources. One shortcoming of this model is its lack of attention to learning outcomes. Exemplary models for assessing the outcomes of student learning are embedded in the INTASC standards for teacher education, which make connections between authentic and performance-based assessment and provide a substantive model for operationalizing state academic performance goals and standards. Other attempts to assess the quality and effectiveness of graduate programs relate to the integration of basic and clinical sciences in the context of case-based learning (Manyon, Feeley, Panzarella, and Servoss, 2003), student attrition and completion rates (Baird, 1993; Lovitt, 2001; Xiao, 1998), alternative modes of student assessment based on content and performance standards (Moore, 1998; Palomba and Banta, 1999), and multiple stakeholder perspectives (Conrad, Haworth, and Millar, 1993).

In the early 1990s, the higher education community met congressional demands for greater government control with hostility. Bloland (2001) provides a detailed ethnographic account of the creation of CHEA and its efforts to establish its legitimacy as a clearinghouse for accrediting agencies, to define its role on the national, regional, and state levels, and to sustain participation of university presidents. He argues that "accreditation provided a much needed [nongovernmental] process for promoting quality assurance in higher education," serving to protect "the integrity and legitimacy of higher education" (p. 203). As he points out, however, "the goal for accrediting higher education institutions and programs in this time of changing technology and delivery systems remains essentially the same as it has been historically, i.e., quality assurance," although this view is also contested terrain (p. 203). Assessment of student learning outcomes, including the tracking of graduates, the recruitment of qualified faculty, improvement of facilities, and closer ties with employers, necessitates major investments in the infrastructure of higher education at a time when state operating budgets are being tightened. Given the increased competition that universities face from for-profit, publicly traded holding companies such as the Apollo Group, DeVry, and Sylvan Learning Systems, the legitimacy of accrediting agencies presents a disturbing conundrum for CHEA and the higher education community. When combined with regional and state oversight and licensing requirements and the pending reauthorization of the Higher Education Act in 2005, the endgame may be an exercise in bureaucratic overkill. CHEA, which represents about three thousand colleges and universities and more than sixty accrediting organizations, has stated that its members oppose the administration's proposal for a graduation or completion rate standard that ignores the complexity and variety of colleges and universities. The former president of Babson College also argues that "roughly 40 agencies—from acupuncture to veterinary medicine— evaluate programs for one or more of the independent institutions in Massachusetts. Some of [them] in health care, architecture, law, engineering, medicine, [and] social work play an important role in public health and safety. In those instances, monitoring is tied to state exams and licensing and oversight of practitioner organizations" (Dill, 1998, p. 20). He adds, however, that "accreditors, regulators, and professional societies combine powerfully not only to assure quality but [also] to establish turf, protect jobs, status, and incomes," serving as power brokers and "promoters of privilege for specialized faculty on campus" (p. 20).

Whether or not institutions should engage in self-regulation or should be subject to external monitoring and mandated criteria for program approval and continuation has been a source of continued debate. In looking at degree proliferation and specialization as master's programs become narrower, more specialized, and less adaptable to situations and circumstances, the connections between professional status and degree acquisition become more tenuous and comparisons more difficult to make. In middle-level administration and management, for example, common elements or strands may recur in preparing students to assume leadership positions in business, health, arts, education, and public administration, each of which confers a different degree. Moreover, degree programs may be narrowly or broadly conceptualized as disciplinary, problem based, interdisciplinary, or multidisciplinary. This disjuncture between programs is reflected in the professional associations that adhere to standards that assure their status and competitiveness in the marketplace while also fostering outcomes measures that encourage them to be distinctive and to engage with social problems. Furthermore, the situation is exacerbated by institutional preoccupations with marketing mechanisms used by graduate and professional schools to maintain their competitive edge.

State legislative demands for accountability and quality assurance are being linked to tuition increases, financial aid, faculty collective bargaining, and capital expenditures. And the lines are blurring between for-profit and not-for-profit centers of graduate education. The growth of credentialism and the master's degree as social and economic currency can be seen in occupational and physical therapy, civil engineering, teacher education, and accountancy—diverse occupations with vested interests in professionalizing their specialties. These changes gain pragmatic legitimacy in a global society as universities confront greater competition in the marketplace, seek to attract external support and recognition, and counteract the rise of for-profit and virtual universities. For those who study professionalism, these changes also reflect a shift in the trajectory from gatekeeping to credentialism, that is, from restricting the supply of practitioners and striving for positions of public respect and influence to raising the collective mobility and status of occupational groups. To some extent, they also underscore that blurred genres relate not only to academic disciplines but also to the adoption of for-profit marketing strategies by not-for-profit institutions.

Given the worldwide development of capacity for in-country offerings in higher education, the growth of the master's degree will continue throughout this decade. Higher education now operates squarely in the global community, and the impact of technological advances extends to every aspect of the academic enterprise. The master's degree is well on its way to becoming fully professionalized as the professions themselves become more entrepreneurial, competitive, and socially accountable. The boundaries that formerly compartmentalized disciplines into isolated departments have become more permeable and indeterminate with the expansion of knowledge production beyond artificially constructed borders. The professional science master's degree is responsive to this trend. Interdisciplinarity in graduate education builds on academic traditions of the core or general education curriculum, but instead of distribution requirements, faculty adopt thematic approaches to teaching and learning that engage multiple disciplinary perspectives. This process is being made possible by global access to the seemingly infinite resources of telecommunications that now makes it possible to earn entire degrees through interactive online systems. It is also facilitated by a consumerist society that has been acculturated to the significance of the academic degree.

Transformative Technological Advances

Technological progress provides momentum for programmatic innovation and for marketing part-time master's degrees to career changers, employed, and nontraditional student groups. Continuing, general studies, and professional development programs, distance learning networks, and for-profit universities offer a plethora of options for achieving graduate degrees. They also override geographic barriers, making it feasible to enroll students in remote locations. With private and state support, virtual and for-profit universities flourish in this largely unregulated, global environment. Peterson's guides list 130 different types of online master's degrees, with the variety of universities offering these degrees ranging from such research I universities as Stanford University, Duke University, and the University of Maryland to for-profit institutions such as the University of Phoenix and Keller Graduate School of Management. A Web site for online learning advertises online master's degrees in thirty fields ranging from accounting, aviation science, and education to social work, public health, and telecommunications. The majority of these degrees are offered in engineering and business including twenty-eight MBA specializations (World-Wide Learn, 2005). For-profit universities are a growing presence in the distance education market: eighty-nine for-profit institutions offer master's programs. Of that total, eight of the largest publicly traded higher education companies account for a total of ninety-eight master's programs, constituting 25.6 percent of their total degree programs. Jules LaPidus, former president of CGS, has predicted that postbaccalaureate futures will include a turning away from degree programs to certificates offered through alternative modes of system delivery (Kohl and LaPidus, 2000). A recent CGS survey of certificate programs conducted in conjunction with the University Continuing Education Association reports a significant increase in graduate certificates, with the most popular programs in education, social sciences, nursing, information technology, gerontology, and engineering, and a growing number that use distance education (Council of Graduate Schools, 2004, p. 4). It is paradoxical, however, that entrenched hierarchical structures of U.S. research universities persist in this competitive marketplace where profitability rather than reputational rankings is a primary factor.

The meteoric rise of corporate universities and online education demonstrates that the next phase of restructuring may well occur through the deinstitutionalization of the university. In his book *Science in the Private Interest,* Krimsky (2003) observes the impact of technology on multinational organizations and American culture:

> We are in an era where traditional sector boundaries are disappearing. Banks have brokerage businesses; brokers do banking. The entertainment industry owns news broadcasting; news broadcasters have taken to entertainment formats. Farms are used to produce agrichemicals; industrial fermenters are used to manufacture food. Animals are being used to make drugs; drugs are used for entertainment. Government researchers are permitted to form partnerships with companies; companies contribute money to federal research on toxic chemicals. Independent auditing firms, responsible for generating federally mandated accounting data on public corporations, provide consultancies to firms they audit. The world is a little topsy-turvy. Perhaps we shouldn't be surprised to learn that non-profit institutions, like universities, are engaging in aggressive for-profit ventures. It is another example of the convoluted boundaries of institutions. [p. 225]

Krimsky (and other critics) raise questions about the challenges of maintaining scientific integrity when corporate/profit/nonprofit boundaries are also becoming indistinct. He contends that to protect the integrity of institutions from erosion and compromise, they should be prohibited by tradition, law, or regulation from taking on conflicting roles (p. 230). These changes support the argument that credentialism rather than gatekeeping will continue to define graduate and professional education. For those who study professionalism, the outlook for regulation in a deregulatory environment is speculative. Rather than restricting the supply of practitioners and striving for exclusivity and status of an elite group of professionals, universities are now engaged in raising the collective mobility and status of all occupational groups.

Conclusions

A NUMBER OF BOOKS DEAL WITH THE ENTREPRENEURIAL university, its corporate outlook, and the consequences of business-industrial-university partnerships for academic policymaking, for example, *Academic Capitalism and the New Economy* (Slaughter and Rhoades, 2004), *Shakespeare, Einstein, and the Bottom Line* (Kirp, 2003), and *The Future of the City of Intellect* (Brint, 2002). Although these works do not specifically address the master's degree, their critiques of the commodification of higher education reflect developments in master's education. Whereas the arts and sciences had been central to the university mission throughout the twentieth century, it is no longer the case. Professional programs now predominate, influenced by technological advances, corporate cultures, and social welfare programs.

Geographic proximity of universities and workplaces, part-time and weekend courses, employer subsidies, and virtual campuses enhance the marketability of the master's degree. The lack of support for these students has become more problematic as a result of precipitous increases in tuition and lower levels of federal or state aid. Most master's degrees can be implemented at low incremental cost by departments and schools where the necessary expertise already exists at the undergraduate or doctoral level. As a result, departments increasingly configure their programs as B.S.–M.S. or M.S.–Ph.D. or the equivalent. Adjunct and non-tenure-track faculty with practitioner expertise and access to industrial and relevant organizational facilities are used in greater numbers to extend the faculty roster and to staff clinical studies and internships. Paralleling tuition trends in medical and law schools, some master's programs, such as the M.B.A., may command higher tuition and fees as a result of their reputation for delivering higher compensation to graduates. For students, the master's is a short-term commitment of one to two years, offering the potential for higher salaries, more job opportunities, and greater technical proficiency. In contrast, implementing the doctorate is a costly venture, necessitating significant fellowship support, strong research faculty and libraries, and, depending on the discipline, enhanced physical space and equipment.

The fundamental breakthroughs in the sciences and the central role of industrial research in biotechnology and related fields raise many issues regarding intellectual property, technology transfer, and venture capital financing (Powell and Owen-Smith, 2002). Undoubtedly, postbaccalaureate futures result in rapid growth with little regulation and a variety of modes of program delivery driven by market forces rather than public policy (Callan and Finney, 2000). It is in this context that the professional master's degree is evolving as an entrepreneurial credential with the potential to alter the direction of graduate education in the sciences. Beyond the sciences, the predominance of professional master's degrees in the social sciences, humanities, and specialized fields indicates not only a different mission for graduate education but also a new direction for the creation and advancement of knowledge.

The production of large numbers of master's candidates is a relatively recent phenomenon in the history of higher education, one that the United States has successfully exported to the European Union, Asia, and Australia. It is implicit in the culture of professionalism and gained credence from the expansion of federal support for graduate education in the 1960s and from the role of the state in linking public higher education to regional economic development. It is only in recent decades that the egalitarian mission of postsecondary education has been extended to graduate and professional schools. Adding to the complexity of expanding this mission to master's education is the development of quality assurance through accreditation, licensure, and ongoing professional development. Faculty and deans need to extend their institutional dialogues to their various clienteles inside and outside the academy, reframing questions about the multiple meanings and purposes of master's education and seeking new directions that restructure the entrenched hierarchies of graduate and professional education. Academic leaders cannot afford to ignore a number of critical issues that remain unresolved in current policy proposals:

- The implications of reconfiguring master's education outside existing organizational structures and the tensions of crossing borders and eradicating boundaries;
- The amorphous nature of interdisciplinarity in the taxonomies and classification systems through which enrollment, degree, and curriculum data are aggregated (and disaggregated);
- The ambiguous relationship between the master's, first-professional degree, and the doctorate in the hierarchy of academic and professional degrees;
- The contested role of accountability for institutions operating in an unregulated global environment;
- The impact on master's education of profitability in a competitive higher education marketplace now being altered by for-profit, corporate, and Internet universities;
- The influential role of credentialism that permeates academic and popular culture and raises questions about degree devaluation and quality assurance;
- The hollow tradition of conferring honorary degrees to reward major donors rather than as evidence of academic and professional achievement.

Higher education now operates squarely in the global community, and the impact of technology extends to every aspect of the academic enterprise. The master's degree is becoming fully professionalized as the professions themselves become more entrepreneurial, competitive, and socially accountable. The boundaries that formerly compartmentalized disciplines into isolated departments have become more permeable and indeterminate as the production of knowledge expands beyond artificially constructed borders. And, not to be overlooked in a nation that has just given corporate tax breaks to multinational corporations, the master's degree is one of American higher education's most successful exports. Based on the author's research on programmatic innovations in graduate education, it is evident that the master's degree will continue its inexorable path to professionalization and will predictably take its place as the academic degree of choice by students, employers, and the state.

Notes

1. The author's research on the master's degree has been informed by studies of its origin and development in European universities, its adoption by American higher education in the nineteenth century, its expansion throughout the past one hundred years in the United States, and its influence on international higher education (Berelson, 1960; Glazer, 1986; Conrad, Haworth, and Millar, 1993).

2. Data on enrollments and degrees are derived primarily from the Integrated Postsecondary Education Data Systems compiled by NCES and *Professional Women and Minorities* compiled by the Commission on Professionals in Science and Technology (Babco and Bell, 2004).

3. First-professional degrees are generally defined as postbaccalaureate degrees of at least three years in duration that earn the recipient the title of "doctor": medicine (M.D.), chiropractic (D.C. or D.C.M.), dentistry (D.D.S. or D.M.D.), optometry (O.D.), osteopathic medicine (D.O.), pharmacy (D.Pharm.), podiatry (Pod.D. or D.P.M.), veterinary medicine (D.V.M.), law (J.D.), and theology (M.Div., M.H.L., or B.D.).

4. This new degree to prepare college faculty to teach liberal arts disciplines, which had been initiated at Carnegie Mellon University in 1969, gained support from four constituent groups: the Carnegie Commission on Higher Education, the Carnegie Corporation, the professional associations, and state higher education coordinating boards, which were motivated by their mutual interest in curbing expansion of the Ph.D., their desire to influence academic change in graduate education, and their ability to provide the requisite resources. The failure of this experiment can be attributed to increased specialization in doctoral education, the perception that alternative degrees lacked status and prestige, and the resurgence of the teaching-learning movement in research universities. For a full discussion of this degree, see Glazer, 1993.

5. The Council of Graduate Schools publishes policy documents to guide faculty and administrators in the organization and administration of graduate schools and the development and assessment of master's and doctoral education. For revised and updated

policy statements on master's education in the United States, see Borchert (1994), and Borchert and Sims (2005).

6. The official Web site for the Bologna process, http://www.bologna-bergen2005.no, contains the text of the declaration, the outcomes of biannual meetings, and details of work in progress. See also *Bologna: A Dream to Reality,* a special issue of the *Times Higher Education Supplement* (April 1, 2005), published one month prior to the 2005 Bergen (Norway) summit.

7. See also "The Business of Business Schools" (Graduate Management Admissions Council, 2001), which analyzes and critiques the ranking systems of business schools by four publications.

8. The New York State Board of Regents offers a third option to smaller education programs, the Regents Accreditation of Teacher Education, in recognition of the fact that departments housed in liberal arts colleges, for example, might not qualify for accreditation using NCATE or TEAC standards that are designed primarily for freestanding schools of education.

9. A conference, *Competencies and Credentials for Training History Professionals,* sponsored by AHA and the Johnson Foundation, brought together representatives of professional associations in history and allied fields at the Wingspread Conference Center in Racine, Wisconsin, May 16–18, 2005, for the purpose of discussing standards and outcomes for master's-level programs in the historical profession and allied fields, including history education, archival studies, public history, and arts administration.

References

Abbott, A. (2001). *Chaos of disciplines.* Chicago: University of Chicago Press.

Abbott, D. M. (1998). *Geologic ethics and professional practices 1987–1997.* Arvada, CO: American Institute of Professional Geologists.

Albrecht, W. S., and Sack, R. J. (2000). *Accounting education: Charting the course through a perilous future.* Retrieved January 16, 2003, from http://www.aicpa.org.

Allen, I. E., and Seaman, J. (2004). *Entering the mainstream: The quality and extent of online education in the United States, 2003 and 2004.* Boston: Sloan Consortium.

Alsop, R. (2004, September 22). And the winners are . . . . *The Wall Street Journal: The Journal Report,* R1–R10.

American Chemical Society. (2003). CPT home page: The master's degree in chemistry. *Chemistry.org,* 1–5. Retrieved January 28, 2003, from http://www.acs.org.

American Institute of Certified Public Accountants. (2004). Frequently asked questions. Retrieved November 17, 2004, from http://www.aicpa.org/nolimits/become/150hr/150her/150faq.htm.

American Society of Civil Engineers. (2004a). *ASCE policy statement: Academic prerequisites for licensure and professional practice.* Reston, VA: American Society of Civil Engineers.

American Society of Civil Engineers. (2004b). *Civil engineering BOK for the 21st century: Preparing the civil engineer for the future.* Reston, VA: American Society of Civil Engineers.

Association for Practical and Professional Ethics. (2004). *Study opportunities in practical and professional ethics.* Retrieved November 30, 2004, from http://www.indiana.edu.

Association for Specialized & Professional Accreditation. (2005). Retrieved September 11, 2005, from http://www.aspa-usa.org.

Association of American Universities. (1910). The degree of Master of Arts. *Journal of Proceedings and Addresses, 12,* 34–50.

Association of American Universities. (1945). The Master's Degree. *Journal of Proceedings and Addresses, 46,* 111–125.

Association of American Universities. (2004, November). Press release: New survey indicates apparent decline in new enrollments of international graduate students in US universities. Retrieved December 15, 2004, from http://www.aau.org.

Association of International Educators. (2004, November). *Survey of foreign student and scholar enrollment and visa trends for Fall 2004.* Retrieved December 2, 2004, from http://www.nafsa.org.

Association to Advance Collegiate Schools of Business. (2004, January). *Eligibility procedures and accreditation standards for business accreditation.* St. Louis: AACSB International. Retrieved November 30, 2004, from http://www.aacsb.edu.

Babco, E., and Bell, N. (2004). *Professional women and minorities: A total human resource data compendium* (15th ed.). Washington, DC: Commission on Professionals in Science and Technology.

Baerwald, T. (2003). View from the National Science Foundation: What is happening and the mechanics of how interdisciplinary research works. In N. E. Bell (Ed.), *Mapping academic disciplines to a multi-disciplinary world* (pp. 5–25). Proceedings of an NSF/CPST Professional Societies Workshop, May 7, 2003. Retrieved electronically October 15, 2003, from http://www.cpst.org.

Baird, L. (Ed.). (1993). *Increasing graduate student retention and degree attainment.* San Francisco: Jossey-Bass.

Becher, T., and Trowler, P. R. (2001). *Academic tribes and territories: Intellectual enquiry and the cultural disciplines* (2nd ed.). Buckingham, UK: Society for Research into Higher Education and Open University Press.

Bender, T., Katz, P. M., Palmer, C., and the AHA Committee on Graduate Education. (2004). *The education of historians for the twenty-first century.* Urbana: University of Illinois Press.

Berelson, B. (1960). *Graduate education in the United States.* New York: McGraw-Hill.

Blackstone, T. (2005, April 1). Nothing to fear but fear itself. Bologna: A dream to reality. *Times Higher Education Supplement 2.* Retrieved May 1, 2005, from http://www.thes.co.uk.

Bledstein, B. J. (1976). *The culture of professionalism: The middle class and the development of higher education in America.* New York: Norton.

Bloland, H. G. (2001). *Creating the Council for Higher Education Accreditation (CHEA).* Phoenix: American Council on Education/Oryx Press.

Bonner, T. N. (2002). *Iconoclast: Abraham Flexner and a life in learning.* Baltimore: Johns Hopkins University Press.

Borchert, M. A. (1994). *Master's education: A guide for faculty and administrators. A policy statement.* Washington, DC: Council of Graduate Schools.

Borchert, M. A., and Sims, L. B. (2005). *Master's education: A guide for faculty and administrators.* Washington, DC: Council of Graduate Schools.

Bourner, T., Bowden, R. and Laing, S. (2001). Professional doctorates in England. *Studies in Higher Education, 26*(1), 65–83.

Bowen, H. R. (1953). Graduate education in economics (Part 2). *American Economic Review Supplement, 43*(4), 1–223.

Boxer, M. J. (1998). *When women ask the questions: Creating women's studies in America.* Baltimore: Johns Hopkins University Press.

Brint, S. (1994). *In an age of experts: The changing role of professionals in politics and public life.* Princeton, NJ: Princeton University Press.

Brint, S. (Ed.). (2002). *The future of the city of intellect: The changing American university.* Stanford, CA: Stanford University Press.

Brown, E. R. (1979). *Rockefeller medicine men: Medicine and capitalism in America.* Berkeley: University of California Press.

Burrage, M., Jarausch, K., and Siegrist, H. (1990). An actor-based framework for the study of the professions. In M. Burrage and R. Torstendahl (Eds.), *Professions in theory and history: Rethinking the study of the professions* (pp. 203–225). London: Sage Publications.

California Council on Science and Technology. (2005). *An industry perspective of the professional science master's degree in California.* Riverside: California Council on Science and Technology.

Callan, P. M., and Finney, J. E. (2000). Higher education's changing contours: The policy implications of an emerging system. In K. Kohl and J. LaPidus (Eds.), *Postbaccalaureate futures* (pp. 216–230). Washington, DC: American Council on Education/Oryx Press.

Carmichael, O. (1961). *Graduate education: A critique and a program.* New York: Harper and Row.

Carnegie Foundation for the Advancement of Teaching. (2001). *The Carnegie Classification of Institutions of Higher Education, 2000.* Menlo Park, CA: Carnegie Foundation for the Advancement of Teaching.

Carnegie Task Force on Teaching as a Profession. (1986). *A nation prepared: Educating teachers for the 21st century.* Washington, DC: Carnegie Forum on Education and the Economy.

Choy, S. P., and Geis, S. (2002). *Student financing of graduate and professional education, 1999–2000* (NCES 2002166). Washington, DC: National Center for Educational Statistics.

Clark, S. (2002). Weatherhead starting bioscience MBA program. *Crain's Cleveland Business, 23*(42), 25.

ClassesUSA. (n.d.). *Online master's degree programs from colleges and universities.* Retrieved November 25, 2004, from http://www.classesusa.com/featuredschools/programs/featured_masters.cfm.

Claudy, N. H., and Keane, C. M. (2003, August). *An assessment of geoscience master's degree programs in the United States* (unpublished report). Washington, DC: American Geological Institute.

Coats, A. W. (1992). Changing perceptions of American graduate education in economics, 1953–1991. *Journal of Economic Education, 23*(4), 341–352.

Cohen, S. (2000). Marketing the MPA degree: The case of the executive MPA program at Columbia University's School of International Affairs and Public Administration. Retrieved on April 2, 2005, from http://www.columbia.edu/sc32/marketing.html.

College of Continuing Studies. (2005). *Master of professional studies.* Storrs: University of Connecticut. Retrieved July 19, 2005, from http://continuingstudies.uconn.edu/mps/.

Collins, R. (1979). *The credential society: A historical sociology of education and stratification.* Orlando, FL: Academic Press.

Collins, R. (1990). Changing conceptions in the sociology of the professions. In R. Torstendahl and M. Burrage (Eds.), *The formation of professions: Knowledge, state and strategy* (pp. 11–23). London: Sage Publications.

Collins, R. (2002). Credential inflation and the future of universities. In S. Brint (Ed.), *The future of the city of intellect* (pp. 23–46). Stanford, CA: Stanford University Press.

Commission on Excellence in Education. (1983). *A nation at risk: The imperative for educational reform.* Washington, DC: Commission on Excellence in Education.

Commission on Higher Education of the Middle States Association of Colleges and Schools. (1979). The assessment of quality of master's programs. *Proceedings.* College Park: University of Maryland. (ED 196 960)

Committee on Science, Engineering, and Public Policy. (1995). *Reshaping the graduate education of scientists and engineers.* Washington, DC: National Academy Press.

Conrad, C. F., and Haworth, J. G. (1997). *Emblems of quality in higher education: Developing and sustaining high-quality programs.* Needham Heights, MA: Allyn & Bacon.

Conrad, C. F., Haworth, J. G., and Millar, S. B. (1993). *A silent success: Master's education in the United States.* Baltimore: Johns Hopkins University Press.

Council for Higher Education Accreditation. (2003). *Fact sheet #1: Profile of accreditation.* Washington, DC: Council for Higher Education Accreditation. Retrieved November 24, 2003, from http://www.chea.org.

Council of Graduate Schools. (1976). *The master's degree: A policy statement.* Washington, DC: Council of Graduate Schools.

Council of Graduate Schools. (2004, August/September). Data sources: Recent findings on postbaccalaureate certificate programs. *CGS Communicator, 4,* 11.

Crainer, S., and Dearlove, D. (1999). *Gravy training: Inside the business of business schools.* San Francisco: Jossey-Bass.

Dahms, A. S. (2001a). Biotechnology education: Editorial. *Biochemistry and Molecular Biology Education, 29,* 121–122.

Dahms, A. S. (2001b). The U.S. biotechnology industry: The importance of workforce quality in the maintenance of corporate competitive advantage. *Biochemistry and Molecular Biology Education, 29,* 206–208.

Dahms, A. S. (2003). Possible road maps for workforce development in biocommerce clusters, including institutions of higher education. *Biochemistry and Molecular Biology Education, 31*(3), 197–202.

Daly, E. (2005, March 28). Columbia plans 2nd masters in journalism. *New York Times,* B6.

Daniel, E. H., and Saye, J. D. (2003). *ALISE Library and Information Science Education Statistical Report 2003.* Retrieved December 10, 2004, from http://ils.unc.edu/ALISE/2003.contents.htm.

Darling-Hammond, L. (1998, May). *Doing what matters most: Investing in quality teaching.* A discussion sponsored by California Education Policy Seminar and the California State University Institute for Educational Reform. Sacramento:

CSU Institute for Education Reform. Retrieved December 22, 2004, from http://www. CSU.edu.

Demyan, B. (2003, Summer). A master's degree for the 21st century. *Science Record,* pp. 14–16.

Dewey, G. (2003, April). *Professional masters in the postgenomic era.* Keck Graduate Institute of Applied Life Sciences. PowerPoint presentation at annual meeting of the American Educational Research Association, San Diego, CA.

Dill, W. R. (1998). Specialized accreditation: An idea whose time has come? Or gone? *Change, 30*(4), 18–25.

Directorate for Engineering. (2005, June). *Strategic directions for engineering research, innovation, and education.* Arlington, VA: National Science Foundation. Retrieved July 20, 2005, from www.nsf.gov.

Dogan, M., and Pahre, R. (1990). *Creative marginality: Innovation at the intersections of social sciences.* Boulder, CO: Westview Press.

Evangelauf, J. (1989, May 10). Accounting educators plan to update curriculum, debate tighter entrance requirements for CPA's. *Chronicle of Higher Education,* p. A31.

Feder, B. J. (2004, October 24). Tiny ideas coming of age. *New York Times: Week in Review,* p. 12.

Flaherty, J. (2004, April 25). The nontraditionalists. The alternative universe: A guide. *New York Times: Education Life,* p. 30.

Flexner, A. (1910). *Medical education in the United States and Canada.* Bulletin 4. New York: Carnegie Foundation for the Advancement of Teaching.

Freedman, J. (2003). *Liberal education and the public interest.* Iowa City: University of Iowa Press.

Freidson, E. (1994). *Professionalism reborn: Theory, prophecy and policy.* Cambridge, MA: Polity Press.

Froment, E. (2005, April 1). Major milestone on our road to reform. Bologna: A dream to reality. *Times Higher Education Supplement 2.* Retrieved May 1, 2005, from www.thes.co.uk.

Geertz, C. (1983). *Local knowledge: Further essays in interpretive anthropology.* New York: Basic Books.

Geiger, R. L. (1986). *To advance knowledge: The growth of American research universities, 1900–1940.* New York: Oxford University Press.

Gerald, D., and Hussar, W. J. (Eds.). (2003, October). *Projections of education statistics to 2013.* Washington, DC: National Center for Education Statistics.

Gibbons, M., and others. (1994). *The new production of knowledge: The dynamics of science and research in contemporary societies.* Beverly Hills, CA: Sage.

Gitlow, A. (1995). *New York University's Stern School of Business: A centennial retrospective.* New York: New York University Press.

Glazer, J. S. (1986). *The master's degree: Tradition, diversity, innovation.* ASHE-ERIC Report No. 6. Washington, DC: George Washington University.

Glazer, J. S. (1993). *A teaching doctorate: The doctor of arts, then and now.* Washington, DC: American Association of Higher Education.

Glazer-Raymo, J. (1999). *Shattering the myths: Women in academe.* Baltimore: Johns Hopkins University Press.

Glazer-Raymo, J. (2001). The fragmented paradigm: Women, tenure, and schools of education. In W. G. Tierney (Ed.), *Faculty work in schools of education: Rethinking roles and rewards in the twenty-first century* (pp. 169–188). Albany: State University of New York Press.

Goldhaber, D., Perry, D., and Anthony, E. (2004). The national board for professional teaching standards (NBPTS) process: Who applies and what factors are associated with NBPTS certification? *Educational Evaluation and Policy Analysis, 26*(4), 259–280.

Gordon, R., and Howell, J. E. (1959). *Higher education for business.* New York: Columbia University Press.

Graduate Management Admissions Council. (2001). The business of business schools. *Selections, 1*(2).

Graff, G. (1992). *Beyond the culture wars: How teaching the conflicts can revitalize American education.* New York: W. W. Norton.

Guillory, J. (2000). The system of graduate education. *PMLA, 115*(5), 1154–1163.

Gumport, P. (2002). *Academic pathfinders: Knowledge creation and feminist scholarship.* Westport, CT: Greenwood Press.

Hansen, W. L. (1990). Educating and training new economics Ph.D.s: How good a job are we doing? *American Economic Review, 80*(2), 437–444.

Hansen, W. L. (1991, September). The education and training of economics doctorates: Major findings of the Executive Secretary of the American Economic Association's Commission on Graduate Education in Economics. *Journal of Economic Literature, 29,* 1054–1087.

Henry, C. (2002, January 7). Careers in bioinformatics. Field not significantly affected by economic downturn, but qualified people still hard to find. *Chemical and Engineering News, 80.* Retrieved February 1, 2003, from http://pubs.acs.org/cen/.

Henry, L. L. (1995). *Early NASPAA history. National Association of Schools of Public Affairs and Administration (NASPAA),* 1–20. Retrieved November 16, 2004, from http://www.naspaa.org/history.asp.

Hill, C. (2005, April). Cambridge's Centre for International Studies: Viewing the world from Mill Lane. *Cambridge in America Newsletter,* 8, 18.

Himmelfarb, G. (1994). *On looking into the abyss: Untimely thoughts on culture and society.* New York: Knopf.

Hoffer, T. B., and others. (2003). *Doctorate recipients from United States universities: Summary report 2002.* Chicago: National Opinion Research Center, University of Chicago.

Holstein, W. G. (2004, October 24). Asking future M.B.A.'s to find the red flags. *New York Times,* p. 10.

Holmes Group. (1986). *Tomorrow's teachers.* East Lansing, MI: Holmes Group.

Holmes Group. (1995). *Tomorrow's schools of education.* East Lansing, MI: Holmes Group.

Howe, B. J. (1993). State of the state of teaching public history. *Teaching History, 18*(2), 51–58.

Isenberg, J. P. (2003, February). *Using national board standards to redesign master's degrees for teachers: A guide for institutions of higher education.* Washington, DC: National Board for Professional Teaching Standards. Retrieved March 1, 2005, from http://www.nbpts.org.

Ivie, R., and Stowe, K. (2003, March). Physics bachelors with master's degrees. *AIP Report.* College Park, MD: American Institute of Physics.

Jobbins, D. (2005, April 1). Introduction to Bologna: A dream to reality. *Times Higher Education Supplement 2.* Retrieved May 1, 2005, from www.thes.co.uk.

Kantz, J. W. (2004, December). *Use of a web-based Delphi for identifying critical components of a professional science master's program in biotechnology.* Ph.D. dissertation, College Station, Texas A&M University.

Katz, P. M. (2003a, February). AHA receives Ford Foundation grant to investigate master's degrees. *Perspectives Online.* Retrieved November 4, 2003, from http://www.theaha.org/perspectives/issues/2003/0302/0302aha1.cfm.

Katz, P. M. (2003b). *Public history employers: What do they want?* Washington, DC: American Historical Association. Retrieved May 27, 2004, from http://www.historians.org/perspectives/issues/2003.

Katz, P. M. (2005). *Retrieving the master's degree from the dustbin of history.* Washington, DC: American Historical Association.

Keck Graduate Institute. (2004). Master of Bioscience: A professional degree. Retrieved December 1, 2004, from http://www.kgi.edu/mbscu.

Kernan, A. (Ed.). (1997). *What's happened to the humanities?* Princeton, NJ: Princeton University Press.

Kirp, D. (2003). *Shakespeare, Einstein, and the bottom line: The marketing of higher education.* Cambridge, MA: Harvard University Press.

Klein, J. T. (1990). *Interdisciplinarity: History, theory, and practice.* Detroit: Wayne State University Press.

Klein, J. T. (1993). Blurring, cracking, and crossing: Permeation and the fracturing of discipline. In E. Messer-Davidow, D. R. Shumway, and D. J. Sylvan (Eds.), *Knowledges: Historical and critical studies in disciplinarity* (pp. 185–211). Charlottesville: University Press of Virginia.

Klein, J. T. (2000). A conceptual vocabulary of interdisciplinary science. In P. Weingart and N. Stehr (Eds.), *Practising interdisciplinarity* (pp. 3–25). Toronto: University of Toronto Press.

Knight, P. T. (1997). Learning, teaching and curriculum in taught master's courses. In P. T. Knight (Ed.), *Masterclass: Learning, teaching and curriculum in taught master's degrees* (pp. 1–16). London: Cassell.

Kohl, K. J., and LaPidus, J. (Eds.). (2000). *Postbaccalaureate futures: New markets, resources, credentials.* Washington, DC: American Council on Education/Oryx Press.

Krimsky, S. (2003). *Science in the private interest.* Cambridge, MA: MIT Press.

Kumar, D. D. (2003, January). Trends in postsecondary science in the United States. *Annals, AAPSS, 585,* 124–133.

Larson, M. S. (1979). *The rise of professionalism: A sociological analysis.* Berkeley: University of California Press.

Leicht, K. T., and Fennell, M. L. (2001). *Professional work: A sociological approach.* Malden, MA: Blackwell.

Leiter, B. (2004). M.A. programs in philosophy. *The philosophical gourmet report.* Retrieved May 5, 2005, from http://www.philosophicalgourmet.com/maprog.htm.

Linkon, S. L. (2005, March). Beyond different boundaries: American studies and public engagement. *Beyond interdisciplinarity: The new goals of American studies programs. American Studies Association Newsletter.* Retrieved May 12, 2005, from http://www.georgetown.edu/crossroads/AmericanStudiesAssn/newsletter/current/Linkon.htm.

Lorange, P. (2002). *New vision for management education: Leadership challenges.* Amsterdam: Pergamon.

Lorden, J., and Slimowitz, J. (2003). Will today's innovations in graduate education meet the challenges of the future? National Science Foundation workshop held May 19–20, 2003. Retrieved December 1, 2003, from www.nsf.gov/dge/InnovMTG.htm.

Lovitt, B. E. (2001). *Leaving the ivory tower: The causes and consequences of departure from doctoral study.* Lanham, MD: Rowman & Littlefield.

Manyon, A. T., Feeley, T. H., Panzarella, K. J., and Servoss, T. J. (2003). Development of an assessment tool measuring medical students' integration of scientific knowledge and clinical communication skills. *Assessment Update, 15*(1), 1–2, 14–15.

May, E. R., and Blaney, D. G. (1981). *Careers for humanists.* New York: Academic Press.

McCoy, J. P., and Milkman, M. I. (1995). Master's degree in economics: Missions and methods. *Journal of Economic Education, 26*(2), 156–175.

Merrill, S. A. (Ed.). (2001). *Trends in federal support of research and graduate education.* Washington, DC: National Academy Press.

Merritt, J. (2004, October 18). The best B-schools. *Business Week,* pp. 62–94.

Modern Language Association Ad Hoc Committee on the Professionalization of Ph.D.s. (2003). *Professionalization in perspective.* Retrieved November 1, 2003, from http://www.mla.org/professionalization.

Moore, R. A. (1998). Helping teachers define and develop authentic assessment and evaluation practices. *Assessment Update, 10*(3), 3, 10, 11.

National Association of Schools of Public Affairs and Administration. (2004). *NASPAA milestones.* Retrieved November 20, 2004, from http://www.naspaa.org/about_naspaa/milestones.asp.

National Council for History Education. (2000). *Building a history curriculum: Guidelines for teaching history in schools* (rev. 2nd ed.). Westlake, OH: Author.

National Research Council. (2003). *Assessing research doctorate programs: A methodology study.* Washington, DC: National Academy of Sciences. Retrieved March 14, 2005, from www.nationalacademies.org/bhew/BHEW_ResearchDoctoratesAssessment.

National Unions of Students in Europe. (2003, August). Joint degrees in the context of the Bologna process. *Integrated curricula: Implications and prospects.* Bologna Follow-Up Seminar. Milano: Ministero dell'Istruzione, dell'Universita e della Ricerca Scientifica–Repubblica Italiana.

Neave, G. (2003). The Bologna declaration: Some of the historic dilemmas posed by the reconstruction of the community in Europe's systems of higher education. *Educational Policy, 17*(1), 141–164.

Newman, F., Couturier, L., and Scurry, J. (2004). *The future of higher education: Rhetoric, reality, and the risks of the market.* San Francisco: Jossey-Bass.

Nicholson, S., and Mulvey, P. J. (2002, September). Roster of physics departments with enrollment and degree data, 2001. *AIP Report.* College Park, MD: American Institute of Physics.

Norton, S. D., Hammer, P. W., and Czujko, R. (2001). *Mastering physics for nonacademic careers.* College Park, MD: American Institute of Physics.

Nowotny, H., Scott, P., and Gibbons, M. (2001). *Rethinking science: Knowledge and the public in an age of uncertainty.* London: Polity Press.

Palmer, C. L. (2001). *Work at the boundaries of science: Information and the interdisciplinary research process.* Dordrecht, Netherlands: Kluwer Publishers.

Palomba, C. A., and Banta, T. W. (Eds.). (1999). *Assessment essentials: Planning, implementing, and improving assessment in higher education.* San Francisco: Jossey-Bass.

Palomba, N. A., and Palomba, C. A. (1999). AACSB accreditation and assessment in Ball State University's College of Business. *Assessment Update, 11*(3), 4–13.

Peterson's Guides. (2005). *Peterson's graduate programs in business, education, health, information studies, law, and social work.* Book 6. Lawrenceville, NJ: Thomson Peterson's.

Pierson, F. C. (1959). *The education of American businessmen.* New York: McGraw-Hill.

Powell, W. W., and Owen-Smith, J. (2002). The new world of knowledge production in the life sciences. In S. Brint (Ed.), *The future of the city of intellect* (pp. 107–130). Stanford, CA: Stanford University Press.

Pryse, M. (1999, June). *Defining women's studies scholarship: A statement of the National Women's Studies Association task force on faculty roles and rewards.* College Park, MD: National Women's Studies Association. Retrieved April 1, 2005, from http://www.nwsa.org.

Rifkin, T. (2003). *Public community college faculty.* Retrieved November 17, 2003, from http://www.aacc.nche.edu/.

Riggs, H. (2002). *Inaugural address* [at Keck Graduate Institute]. Retrieved November 22, 2004, from http://www.kgi.edu.

Ronalds, B. F. (1999). Involving industry in university education: The master of oil and gas engineering. *European Journal of Engineering Education, 24*(4), 395–404.

Rubin, E., Bernath, U., and Parker, M. (2004). The master of distance education program: A collaboration between the University of Maryland University College and Oldenburg University. *Journal of Asynchronous Learning Networks, 8*(3), 1–19. Retrieved November 30, 2004, from http://www.sloan-c.org/publications/jaln/v8n3.asp.

Ruch, R. S. (2001). *Higher ed, inc.: The rise of the for-profit university.* Baltimore: Johns Hopkins University Press.

Samudhram, A. (2002, November 21). Advancing bioinformatics research. *Computimes Malaysia,* pp. 1–3.

Sanchez, G. J. (2003). *Mid-year report of the American Studies Association Task Force on Graduate Education.* Retrieved May 12, 2005, from http://www.georgetown.edu/crossroads/ AmericanStudiesAssn/newsletter.

Sanchez, G. J. (2005). Keeping the dance alive: Institutionalization of the crossroads of ethnic and American studies. *Beyond interdisciplinarity: The new goals of American studies programs. American Studies Association Newsletter.* Retrieved July 21, 2005, from http://www. georgetown.edu/crossroads/AmericanStudiesAssn/newsletter/current/Sanchez.

Shafer, W. E., and Kunkel, J. G. (2001). Are 150-hour accounting programs meeting their intended objectives? *Journal of Education for Business, 77*(2), 78–82.

Simmons, C. A. (2002). *New careers, new career paths for science trained professionals* (unpublished report). New York: The Conference Board.

Slaughter, S., and Rhoades, G. (2004). *Academic capitalism and the new economy: Markets, state, and higher education.* Baltimore: Johns Hopkins University Press.

Snell, L. (1965). The master's degree. In E. Walters (Ed.), *Graduate education today* (pp. 74–102). Washington, DC: American Council on Education.

Snyder, T., Tan, A. G., and Hoffman, C. M. (Eds.). (2004). *Digest of education statistics 2003.* Washington, DC: National Center for Education Statistics.

Society of American Archivists. (2002). *Guidelines for a graduate program in archival studies.* Retrieved May 19, 2005, from http://www.archivists.org/prof-education/ ed_guidelines.asp.

Solmon, L. C., Kent, L., Ochsner, N. L., and Hurwicz, M. (1981). *Underemployed Ph.D.'s.* Lexington, MA: Lexington Books.

Spinelli, G. (2003). Concepts and models in integrated programmes at master's level. *Integrated curricula: Implications and prospects.* Bologna Follow-up Seminar. Milano: Ministero dell'Istruzione, dell'Universita e della Ricerca Scientifica–Repubblica Italiana.

Spurr, S. H. (1970). *Academic degree structures: Innovative approaches. Principles of reform in degree structures in the United States.* Berkeley, CA: Carnegie Foundation for the Advancement of Teaching.

Stacy, A. M. (2000). The graduate student in the dual role of student and teacher. In *Graduate education in the chemical sciences: Issues for the 21st century* (pp. 73–90). Chemical Sciences Roundtable, National Research Council. Washington, DC: National Academy Press.

State Education Department. (1972). *Master's degrees in the state of New York, 1969–70.* Albany: University of the State of New York.

Storr, R. J. (1953). *The beginning of graduate education in America.* Chicago: University of Chicago Press.

Syverson, P. (2004). Press release: Council of Graduate Schools survey finds widespread declines in international graduate student applications to U.S. graduate schools for fall 2004. Washington, DC: Council of Graduate Schools.

Syverson, P. D., and Sims, L. B. (2003). *Professional master's programs in the social sciences: Current status and future possibilities.* Unpublished report on a research project funded by the Ford Foundation, Council of Graduate Schools, Washington, DC.

Tauch, C. (2002). Master degrees in the European higher education area. In C. Tauch and A. Rauhvargers (Eds.), *Survey on master degrees and joint degrees in Europe* (pp. 7–26). Brussels: European University Association.

Thelin, J. (2004). *A history of American higher education.* Baltimore: Johns Hopkins University Press.

Thompson, B. (2000). *Guide to graduate work in women's studies* (3d ed.). College Park, MD: National Women's Studies Association.

Thorne, P. (1997). Standards and quality in taught master's programmes. In P. T. Knight (Ed.), *Masterclass* (pp. 16–27). London: Cassell.

Thornton, R. J., and Innes, J. T. (1988). The status of master's programs in economics. *Journal of Economic Perspectives, 2*(1), 171–178.

Thurgood, L. (2004, June). Graduate enrollment in science and engineering fields reaches new peak; first-time enrollment of foreign students declines. *InfoBrief: Science Resources Statistics.* Arlington, VA: National Science Foundation. Retrieved July 16, 2004, from http://www.nsf.gov/sbe/srs/.

Thurow, L. (2003). *Fortune favors the bold: What we must do to build a new and lasting global prosperity.* New York: Harper Business.

Turley, J. P. (1996). Toward a model for nursing informatics. *Journal of Nursing Scholarship, 28*(4), 309–313.

University of California Office of Planning and Analysis. (1999). *Educating the next generation of Californians in a research university context: University of California graduate and undergraduate enrollment planning through 2010.* Appendix 2. Workforce projections and job market trends for graduate and professional degree recipients (pp. 35–43). Berkeley: Office of the President.

U.S. Department of Education. (2004, October). *A guide to education and the No Child Left Behind Act.* Retrieved May 10, 2005, from http://www.ed.gov/nclb/landing.jhtml.

Wasserman, E. (2000). Graduate education in the chemical sciences. *Graduate education in the chemical sciences: Issues for the 21st century* (pp. 18–26). Chemical Sciences Roundtable, National Research Council. Washington, DC: National Academy Press.

Whitsonant, R. C., and Philley, J. C. (1997, May). Registration and testing of practicing geologists: Implications for academic programs. *Geologic ethics and professional practices, 1987–1997* (pp. 104–108). Arvado, CO: American Institute of Professional Geologists.

Wiess School of Natural Sciences. (2005). Centers and institutes at Rice University. Retrieved April 5, 2005, from http://natsci.rice.edu.

Wikle, T. A., and Finchum, G. A. (2003). The emerging GIS degree landscape. *Computers, Environment, and Urban Systems, 27*(2), 107–122.

Wilensky, H. L. (1964). The professionalization of everyone? *American Journal of Sociology, 70*(2), 137–158.

Wilkinson, S. (2002). Industry's wish list for academia. *Chemical and Engineering News, 80*(37), 34.

Wilson, R. (2005). Deep thought, quantified. *Chronicle of Higher Education, 51,* 8.

WorldWide Learn. (2005). *Distance learning and online education.* Retrieved July 20, 2005, from http://www.worldwidelearn.com.

Wright, E. (2004). Graduate degrees on the margins: Educational and professional concerns of the MA student. *Journal of the Midwest Modern Language Association, 37*(2), 30–36.

Xiao, B. (1998). *Factors influencing master's degree attainment in business, engineering, health and human sciences, and visual and performing arts.* Paper presented at the annual forum of the Association for Institutional Research, May 17–20, 1998, Minneapolis, MN. (ED 424 807)

Name Index

O

Ochsner, N. L., 77
Owen-Smith, J., 110

P

Pahre, R., 27
Palmer, C., 27, 52
Palomba, C. A., 38, 103
Palomba, N. A., 38
Panzarella, K. J., 103
Parker, M., 31–32
Perry, D., 47
Philley, J. C., 65
Pierson, F. C., 37
Powell, W. W., 110
Pryse, M., 96

R

Rhoades, G., 109
Rifkin, T., 79
Riggs, H., 58
Ronalds, B. F., 73
Rubin, E., 31–32
Ruch, R. S., 40

S

Sack, R. J., 43
Samudhram, A., 56
Sanchez, G. J., 93, 94
Saye, J. D., 30
Scott, P., 2–3, 23
Scurry, J., 100
Seaman, J., 31
Servoss, T. J., 103
Shafer, W. E., 42–43
Siegrist, H., 14
Simmons, C. A., 62
Sims, L. B., 32, 33, 77, 113
Slaughter, S., 109

Slimowitz, J., 52
Snell, L., 79–80
Snyder, T., 2, 27, 45
Solmon, L. C., 77
Spinelli, G., 15
Spurr, S. H., 6, 7, 9,
  10, 34
Stacy, A. M., 67
Storr, R. J., 6
Stowe, K., 69
Syverson, P., 22, 32, 33

T

Tan, A. G., 2, 27, 45
Tappan, H., 6
Tauch, C., 15
Taylor, R., 40
Thelin, J., 7, 8
Thompson, B., 95, 97
Thorne, P., 16
Thornton, R. J., 86
Thurgood, L., 73
Thurow, L., 101
Tobias, S., 60
Trowler, P. R., 14, 101
Turley, J. P., 57

W

Wasserman, E., 68
Weisbuch, R., 78
Whitsonant, R. C., 65
Wikle, T. A., 88, 89
Wilensky, H. L., 12, 13
Wilkinson, S., 67
Wilson, R., 84
Wright, E., 78

X

Xiao, B., 103

Subject Index

E

Economics, 85–88
Education Commission for the States, 47
Education degree, 44–50
Education of Historians for the Twenty-First Century (AHA), 81
Elementary and Secondary Education Act, 80
Empire State College (New York), 30
Engineering, 51–74, 70–73
EU. *See* European Union
EUA. *See* European University Association
European Union (EU), 14, 99
European University Association (EUA), 15, 99

F

Federal Aid, 9–11
Fielding Institute, 30
Financial Times, 28–29
Ford Foundation, 37, 76, 96
Fujitsu, 41
Future of the City of Intellect (Brint), 109

G

Geographic information systems, 60, 88–89
Geologic Ethics and Professional Practices, 1989–1997 (Abbott), 65
George Washington University, 95
Geosciences, 64–66
Globalization, 99–101
Graduate education, professionalizing, 11–14
Graduate Education in Economics (Bowen), 85–86
Graduate Record Examination Board, 11
Graduate Record Examination (GRE), 26
Great Society, 90
Guide to Graduate Work in the United States (Thompson), 95
Guide to Graduate Work in Women's Studies (Thompson), 97

H

Hamline University, 67
Harvard University, 6, 7, 37, 44
Higher Education Act (1968), 90, 91
Higher Education Act (2005), 49, 104
History studies, 79–84
Hitosubashi University (Japan), 41
Holmes Group, 46
Humanistic studies, 77–86

I

Indian Institute of Management, 41
Indiana, 46
INSEAD (European Union), 41
Institute for Management Accountants, 43
Institute for Professional Development, 39
Institute of Medicine, 51
Integrated Graduate Research and Education Traineeship Program, 52
Intel University, 39
Interdisciplinary fields, 92–98
Intergovernmental Personnel Act, 90
International Institute of Management Development (IMD; Lausanne, Switzerland), 40, 41
Interstate New Teacher Assessment and Support Consortium (INTASC), 47–49

J

Johns Hopkins University, 7
Journal of Biochemistry and Molecular Biology Education (COSEPUP), 53

K

Keck Foundation, 64
Master of Bioscience, 58
Keck Graduate Institute (KGI) 58, 59
Keller Graduate School of Management, 40, 106
KGI. *See* Keck Graduate Institute (KGI)

L

Language studies, 77–79
Lauder Institute (Wharton Business School), 41

Lehigh University Satellite Network, 67
Liberal Studies, 92–93
Liechtenstein, 15
Loyola University, 85
Lufthansa, 41

M

Marquette University, 85
Massachusetts Institute of Technology, 56
Master of Bioscience Degree, 57–64
Masterclass (Knight), 16
Master's degree
    conceptualizing, 1–4; evolution of,
        5–22; in selected fields, 1980–1981,
        1990–1991, and 2000–2001, 36
Master's education
    curricular models of, 23–34;
        reframing, 32–34
Master's students
    changing demographics of, 17–22; and
        degrees awarded by field, sex, and
        race or ethnicity, 2001–2002, 20–21;
        percentage distribution of, by gender,
        age, and marital of dependent status,
        1999–2000, 18
Matshushita, 41
McDonald's Hamburger University, 39
McGill University (Canada), 41, 85
Michigan State University, 61, 85
Modern Language Association
    (MLA), 76–78
Morrill Act (1862), 7
Motorola University, 39

N

Nation at Risk, (Commission on
    Excellence in Education), 46
Nation Prepared (Carnegie Task Force on
    Teaching as a Profession), 46
National Academy of Engineering,
    51, 72
National Academy of Sciences, 51
National Aeronautics and Space
    Administration (NASA), 25
National Association of Boards of
    Geology, 65

National Association of Independent
    Colleges and Universities (NAICU), 49
National Association of Schools of Public
    Affairs and Administration, 90, 91
National Association of State Boards of
    Education (NASBE), 49
National Association of State Universities
    and Land-Grant Colleges, 49
National Board for Professional Teaching
    Standards (NBPTS), 47, 48
National Center for Education Statistics
    (NCES), 2, 21, 28, 35, 45, 47
National Center for Geographic
    Information and Analysis, 89
National Council for Accreditation of
    Teacher Education (NCATE), 49
National Council for Examiners for
    Engineering and Surveying, 72
National Council of Teachers of Social
    Studies, 80
National Council on History Education, 80
National Council on Public History, 82–83
National Defense Education Act (1957), 9
National Education Association (NEA), 49
National Endowment for the Humanities
    (NEH), 25
National Governors Association, 47
National Institutes of Health, 25, 100
National Opinion Research Center
    (NORC; University of Chicago), 24–25
National Postsecondary Student Aid Study
    (NPSAS), 17
National Research Council (NRC), 27,
    28, 97
    Panel on Taxonomy and
        Interdisciplinarity, 27
National Science Foundation (NSF), 25,
    26, 52, 53, 71
National Society for Professional
    Engineers, 72
National Survey of Postsecondary
    Faculty, 79
National Unions of Students in
    Europe, 99
NBTS. *See* National Board for Professional
    Teaching Standards

State University of New York, Buffalo, 63
Stony Brook University, 47
Strategic Directions for Engineering Research, Innovation and Education (NSF), 71
Survey of Earned Doctorates, 24–26
Sylvan Learning Systems, 104

T

Teacher Education Accreditation Council (TEAC), 49
Texas A&M University, 55
Times Higher Education supplement, 16
Tomorrow's Schools of Education (Holmes Group), 46
Tomorrow's Teachers (Holmes Group), 46
Transformative Technological Advances, 106–108
Tulane University, 79–80

U

United Kingdom, 14, 15, 39
United States Association for international Development, 90
United States Civil Service Commission, 90
United States Department of Agriculture, 25
United States Department of Education, 25, 46, 49, 80
Universities Without Walls, 4, 30
University Consortium for Geographic Information Science, 89
University Continuing Education Association, 107
University of Arizona, 61, 69
University of California, Los Angeles, 61
University of California, Office of Planning and Analysis, 62
University of Cambridge, 16, 56
University of Central Florida, 67
University of Chicago
    Department of Sociology, 13; National Opinion Research Center, 24–25
University of Cincinnati, 96

University of Colorado, Denver, 67
University of Edinburgh, 89
University of Greenwich, 16
University of Lancaster (United Kingdom), 41
University of Maryland University College, 31–32, 106
University of Massachusetts, 91
    UMass Online, 31
University of Michigan, 6
University of Oldenburg (Germany), 31–32
University of Pennsylvania, 37, 56, 85
University of Phoenix, 39, 106
University of Southern California, 93
University of Texas, Austin, 9–10
University of Texas, Dallas, 89
University of Utah, 91
University of Western Australia, 72
U.S. News & World Report, 28–29

V

Vatican City, 15

W

Wall Street Journal, 43
Weatherhead School of Management, 41
Weiss School of Natural Sciences, 56
West Point, 7
Western Governors University, 30
Western International University, 39
Wharton Business School (University of Pennsylvania), 37, 40
Women's studies, 95–98
Woodrow Wilson Foundation, 78
Woodrow Wilson Project on the Responsive Ph.D., 52, 78
WorldWide Learn, 106

Y

Yale University, 6, 7
    School of Management, 44
Youngstown State University, 94

About the Author

Judith Glazer-Raymo is lecturer and fellow of the higher and postsecondary education program at Teachers College, Columbia University, and professor emerita of education at Long Island University. She is the author of books and articles on graduate and professional education, higher education policymaking, and gender equity. Her long-standing interest in graduate and professional education is exemplified by publication of *The Master's Degree: Tradition, Diversity, Innovation* (1986), a study of the professional Doctor of Arts degree (1993), and articles and book chapters on the professionalization of higher education. Her interest also extends to the evaluation and registration of master's programs and the development of graduate consortia in the arts and sciences. In 2002, at the invitation of the Sloan Foundation's Professional Science Master's Program, she undertook a national review of master's education in the sciences and mathematics. This monograph is partly the result of that review.

She has received the ASHE Research Achievement award (2004), the AERA Willystine Goodsell award (2001), the LIU Trustees Award for Scholarly Achievement (2001), and the AERA Postsecondary Division's Outstanding Publication Award (2000) for *Shattering the Myths: Women in Academe.* She earned a B.A. in English from Smith College and a Ph.D. in higher education from New York University.

About the ASHE Higher Education Reports Series

Since 1983, the ASHE (formerly ASHE-ERIC) Higher Education Report Series has been providing researchers, scholars, and practitioners with timely and substantive information on the critical issues facing higher education. Each monograph presents a definitive analysis of a higher education problem or issue, based on a thorough synthesis of significant literature and institutional experiences. Topics range from planning to diversity and multiculturalism, to performance indicators, to curricular innovations. The mission of the Series is to link the best of higher education research and practice to inform decision making and policy. The reports connect conventional wisdom with research and are designed to help busy individuals keep up with the higher education literature. Authors are scholars and practitioners in the academic community. Each report includes an executive summary, review of the pertinent literature, descriptions of effective educational practices, and a summary of key issues to keep in mind to improve educational policies and practice.

The Series is one of the most peer reviewed in higher education. A National Advisory Board made up of ASHE members reviews proposals. A National Review Board of ASHE scholars and practitioners reviews completed manuscripts. Six monographs are published each year and they are approximately 120 pages in length. The reports are widely disseminated through Jossey-Bass and John Wiley & Sons, and they are available online to subscribing institutions through Wiley InterScience (http://www.interscience.wiley.com).

Call for Proposals

The ASHE Higher Education Report Series is actively looking for proposals. We encourage you to contact one of the editors, Dr. Kelly Ward (kaward@wsu.edu) or Dr. Lisa Wolf-Wendel (lwolf@ku.edu), with your ideas.

Professionalizing Graduate Education

Recent Titles

Volume 28 ASHE-ERIC Higher Education Reports

Back Issue/Subscription Order Form

Copy or detach and send to:

Jossey-Bass, A Wiley Imprint, 989 Market Street, San Francisco CA 94103-1741

Call or fax toll-free: Phone 888-378-2537 6:30AM – 3PM PST; Fax 888-481-2665

Back Issues: Please send me the following issues at $24 each
(Important: please include series abbreviation and issue number.
For example ASHE 28:1)

_____

_____

_____

$ _____   Total for single issues

$ _____   SHIPPING CHARGES: SURFACE   Domestic Canadian

	First Item	$5.00	$6.00
	Each Add'l Item	$3.00	$1.50

For next-day and second-day delivery rates, call the number listed above

Subscriptions   Please ❑ start ❑ renew my subscription to *ASHE Higher Education Reports* for the year 2_____at the following rate:

U.S.	❑ Individual $165	❑ Institutional $175
Canada	❑ Individual $165	❑ Institutional $235
All Others	❑ Individual $213	❑ Institutional $286

❑ Online subscriptions available too!

**For more information about online subscriptions visit
www.interscience.wiley.com**

$ _____   Total single issues and subscriptions (Add appropriate sales tax for your state for single issue orders. No sales tax for U.S. subscriptions. Canadian residents, add GST for subscriptions and single issues.)

❑Payment enclosed (U.S. check or money order only)

❑VISA ❑ MC ❑ AmEx ❑ #_____ Exp. Date _____

Signature _____ Day Phone _____

❑ Bill Me (U.S. institutional orders only. Purchase order required.)

Purchase order # _____

Federal Tax ID13559302   **GST 89102 8052**

Name _____

Address _____

_____

Phone _____ E-mail _____

For more information about Jossey-Bass, visit our Web site at **www.josseybass.com**

ASHE-ERIC HIGHER EDUCATION REPORT IS NOW AVAILABLE ONLINE AT WILEY INTERSCIENCE

What is Wiley InterScience?

Wiley InterScience is the dynamic online content service from John Wiley & Sons delivering the full text of over 300 leading scientific, technical, medical, and professional journals, plus major reference works, the acclaimed Current Protocols laboratory manuals, and even the full text of select Wiley print books online.

What are some special features of Wiley InterScience?

Wiley Interscience Alerts is a service that delivers table of contents via e-mail for any journal available on Wiley InterScience as soon as a new issue is published online.
Early View is Wiley's exclusive service presenting individual articles online as soon as they are ready, even before the release of the compiled print issue. These articles are complete, peer-reviewed, and citable.
CrossRef is the innovative multi-publisher reference linking system enabling readers to move seamlessly from a reference in a journal article to the cited publication, typically located on a different server and published by a different publisher.

How can I access Wiley InterScience?

Visit http://www.interscience.wiley.com.

Guest Users can browse Wiley InterScience for unrestricted access to journal Tables of Contents and Article Abstracts, or use the powerful search engine.
Registered Users are provided with a *Personal Home Page* to store and manage customized alerts, searches, and links to favorite journals and articles. Additionally, Registered Users can view free Online Sample Issues and preview selected material from major reference works.
Licensed Customers are entitled to access full-text journal articles in PDF, with select journals also offering full-text HTML.

How do I become an Authorized User?

Authorized Users are individuals authorized by a paying Customer to have access to the journals in Wiley InterScience. For example, a University that subscribes to Wiley journals is considered to be the Customer.
Faculty, staff and students authorized by the University to have access to those journals in Wiley InterScience are Authorized Users. Users should contact their Library for information on which Wiley journals they have access to in Wiley InterScience.

ASK YOUR INSTITUTION ABOUT WILEY INTERSCIENCE TODAY!